WINNING AT SALES
It's a Lot More MONEY!

ISBN:10-148-2337665
ISBN-13:978-1482337662
LCCN:2013933646

Cover - Logo Design & Published by
Roger W. Breternitz CCht.
&
Vector Studios®

Laguna Niguel Ca.

Website: www.awinnersway.com
Website: www.vectorstudios.com

WINNING AT SALES
It's a Lot More Money!

Reprogram yourself to say and do just the right things to get people to say
YES!

Winning comes from experience, and experience comes from PLAYING.

GET IN THE GAME!

By Roger W. Breterntiz CCht.

FORWARD

This book is directed to all the gifted individuals out there that make their living, or want to make their living from saying just the right things, at the right time, in the right manner to make someone else THINK, it's their idea to buy whatever that person is selling. This is called, "Sales", and it's been going on ever since Eve persuaded Adam to take a bite of that forbidden apple. It was something that he knew he shouldn't do, knew he should stay away from, and something he was told NOT to do. But something got into the picture; something he didn't count on, and it was most likely his first experience with what is called EMOTION. Eve knew exactly where that emotion "Button" was, and didn't bat an eye when she had the chance to not only push it, but jump on it! She was humanity's first "Closer".

Since then, no matter what you do, you're either a seller or a buyer, and these roles keep changing every day. Because the act of successful selling is nothing more than presenting an idea or product in a manner that invokes an emotional response in someone, in turn making them want what is being presented, totally irrespective of the face that they may or may not NEED it. This in turn triggers their "Buy it now" blinking light, and suddenly they're signing the papers, reading their credit card number or reaching for their wallet. This book is about why people do just that, along with causing them to do it more often, and how to make them feel good about it after they do...so they don't cancel their check or dispute their charge card. Sales is one of the highest paid professions if you break it down to an hourly wage, depending upon what you are selling, so you can examine that fact BEFORE you go into sales and calculate what each sale is worth, how much effort you have to go through to get it, and hopefully come up with a decision of what would be the best product for you to sell. This would depend on your knowledge of the product or service, how well you relate to the people who would be your client/customers and an overall "Feeling" of the answer to the question, "How would I like selling xxx to xxx type people". So keep in mind the saying, "Do what you love and you'll never work a day in your life." That's all well and good, you're thinking, but it seems that the photographer job at Playboy magazine (If you're a guy) has just been filled, or the "Private secretary to Donald Trump", job (if you're a woman) has seemed to have passed you by.

Part of this book should have a chapter called "Get real", but for right now I think, IF you're reading it, you just took the first step to getting real in the first place, so we'll just dwell on the reason you bought/or will buy it. MAKING MORE MONEY! No matter what you are selling, you have to like the people you're working with and selling TO. So if you don't like being lied to jerked around, doors slammed in your face, don't pick TELEMARKETING. There's a LOT of money in it, but you have to be a special kind of "GI Joe" of sales, that doesn't mind getting shot at, and shot down, and thrown out the 10th story window of rejection.

Each job in sales has a level of academic background. If you are in a specific sales job of selling ENGINEERING services, then you need a BSME (Bachelor of Science in....ENGINEERING) in the discipline of engineering in which you are selling. On the other hand if you are selling copier supplies like ink and toner, you just need to like being knocked down, told "NO", and keep bouncing back, and no academic background is necessary. Not to cast a shadow on this aspect of selling because I know of several guys selling copier supplies that made $1200 a WEEK! It all comes down to usually one thing, and that's why we're all here. It's about making enough money to be comfortable and enjoy life, on a level higher than you are now...or you wouldn't be reading this.

This publication is designed to teach you things that you didn't know, would have never known, make you more money than you are now making, and with less effort! If you learn (check the definition of learning) one thing that closes one deal that makes you more that 20 bucks, YOU'RE AHEAD. It's like that statement by Oliver Wendell Homes, "*A mind expanded to larger ideas will never return to its original size*." You will have learned it and be able to use it for the rest of your life, always closing more deals and making more MONEY!

DEDICATION

Sales is such a grinding job, day in and day out, and many times, thankless business. So with that in mind, I dedicate this book to the person who has taken it upon themselves to find a "Better way" to rise to the top. It may be rising to the top of their own organization, or taking that organization to the top of the of the heap we call success. At any rate you the reader deserve the firm handshake of "Well done" in your effort to become the best and most efficient salesperson you can be. You have come to the realization that no matter how much experience you have, how many deals you've closed, and how much you THINK you know, in sales, just like in life, you never quit learning.

Once there was a salesman that cost his employer a LOT of money because of not being attuned to one small detail. The initial phase of his termination by his boss started out with the words, *"Your problem is, you don't know how much you don't know!"*

With the purchase of this book you've just declared you DO realize how much you don't know, there is always something to be learned, and that knowledge is the real key to more money, greater efficiency, better decisions, and a more enjoyable life.

This book is dedicated to you the reader and Captain of your own ship, be it a dingy or the Starship Enterprise. So, congratulations on realizing that YOU are the one responsible for closing the deal, attention to the lose ends, and making the client/customer feel as if they have done the "Right thing".

You've realized that no matter what the outcome, you've taken responsibility for your own actions. These are the thoughts, values and mannerisms of the MASTER CLOSER, good luck on becoming one, and remember...JUST DO IT!

READ THIS!

AUTHOR'S NOTE:
It is a known fact that we remember less of what we READ, more of what we HEAR, more of what we SEE, and the retention goes up from there as we incorporate seeing AND hearing, then SEE, HEAR, and DOING. It is for this reason that I have some paragraphs/concepts/text or divisions within chapters *REPEATED.* The repetition is however not word for word, although it has much of the same information stated in different words, or additional explanations. This is in hopes of bringing about greater retention of information imparted, with the idea that if you *RETAIN* it you will *EMPLOY* it, which as you will find out, is the definition of LEARNING!

So, if you read something that you think you've already come across, you probably have, but if reading it again causes you to retain, and USE it, once again you've LEARNED IT.

ACKNOWLEDGMENTS

Winning, it's a Lot More Fun By
Roger W. Breternitz CCht.

NLP – The New Technology of Achievement By
Steve Andreas & Charles Faulkn

The Seven Laws of Money by
Michael Phillips

Formatting – Christina Dury

Table of contents

CHAPTER 1
WHO IS THIS BOOK FOR?

This book was written for people who have always been salespeople. They started out as a 5 year old selling their Mom or Dad the idea that what THEY wanted was more important than what they needed or what their parents intended for them to do...to be...or just to become, and...they were good at it! Later on, that decision might not have been so good, but whatever!

Without formal training they had a way of presenting ideas in their best light, maximizing the positive, minimizing the negative, fudging reality to best suit their cause, and increasing the width of the thin line between right and wrong, good and not so good. Finally they just plain pulled you into their sphere of influence like a spider weaves a web of attraction to the unsuspecting fly that never realizes he's caught until it's too late, or gives up his credit card number.

Then Mom or Pop says, "What did I just agree to?" That's where the term, "Twist him around your little finger", comes from. Have you ever been twisted around someone's little finger? If so, then you know the meaning of a "Master closer".

I am a firm believer that "You can't make a silk purse out of a sow's ear", kind of thinking. You can't teach a lamb how to be a lion and the metaphors go on and on. Some people will never, ever, ever...become a proficient salesperson, and

I've known lots of them that tried when they got fired or laid off their "Regular" job.

I did engineering design for over 22 years and suddenly computer 3D design software came along, I didn't keep up with the new technology and was looking for work for the next few months. So went back to what I could do easily which was, get someone to buy something. I began to realize that the hourly rate was a lot higher, with less work, but more skill. You had to "Like" getting the door "Slammed in your face", and you learned to "Thicken your skin", but guess what, you were laughing all the way to the bank!

Since then I've been through no less than 16 different sales courses taught by people who were suppose to be the top gurus of their profession, selling IPOs (Initial Public Offerings), to FCC licenses, and everything in between. I discovered one major truth, and it all seems to boil down to the same small group of truths. These truths apply to any sales situation, any group of sales prospects, and just about anything someone can dream up to sell to anyone else.

I took the most important of these truths, proverbs, and axioms, to compile this book, and then put in the one thing that no trainer has ever mentioned or even hinted at, in all the sales courses I've been through. What I am referring to are detailed instructions on the use of Neuro-Linguist Programming for achieving rapport, mentally preparing the buyer for the advance closing techniques and the use of these techniques.

How did I get this knowledge? I decided I wanted to learn hypnosis, and then wanted to become a Hypnotherapist, then a Clinical Hypnotherapist, and after 300 hours of instruction opened my office at the place where I received my certifications. Since then I've helped hundreds of people quit smoking, lose weight, and focus their lives toward a more rewarding leap over all the hurdles that were blocking their progress. It was then that they finally crossed the "Goal line" of what they wanted to achieve in life!

This new science of selling is something that will probably be declared illegal to use in sales (if it can be proved as being used) some day because it is so powerful at gaining rapport, and pre-programming someone's inner mind to get the response you want. In general it will make you a smashing success, and save yourself about $1800 in process as opposed to actually going through an NLP course that, by the way, is NOT tailored to the sales arena at all.

It's a form of hypnosis, and mental reprogramming with you as the reprogrammer. There are specific ways that people PREFER to receive and transmit information, much like a radio frequency. If you are not "Transmitting" on the correct frequency to the person you are trying to convince to buy something, they don't hear you, they don't see you, and they don't listen to you. So, it's up to you to find and use this correct frequency when you talk, gesture, stand/sit, and just about any other of your mannerisms you exhibit while in the company of your client/customer. This book is about finding and using that frequency to first of all, get their ATTENTION, then you begin the sales process in a manner that gets results.

When you DO know how to find this magic frequency of "Informational transference" you will have what is called "Rapport", and this is what closes deals, causes someone to "Like" you, and attracts people to you like a magnet. For this you need to know the TRUE definition of hypnosis.

HYPNOSIS: When the mind substitutes imagination and or visualization for reality.

This is when you daydream, and your mind goes into a state imaging an event or projected reality. Suddenly you're 3 miles past your off ramp on the freeway when you are just trying to get home, or there's a flashing red light behind your bumper and you can't understand how you're suddenly going 90 mph. You were HYPNOTIZED, and you did it to yourself, by yourself, all on your own.

In the field of sales an example would be, when you describe the fun and enjoyment someone will have when they go whisking down the road in the car you are trying to sell them. If you can get them to feel the wind in their hair, the surge of acceleration, and their hands on the wheel, BEFORE they take the test drive, you're using hypnosis. The trouble is, without proper instruction, you're using it like a monkey would use a typewriter. Eventually it would type a word, by accident, but not be able to duplicate it, or know what it means. What you will learn from this book is how to FOCUS the power of hypnosis, or projecting reality into "Make believe", and put the client/customer into a state of "Post-ownership" of your product or service. They will experience the FEELING of **already** having, using, experiencing the pleasure of *OWNING* the product or service, BEFORE they buy it.

You have just projected in front of that person a new reality, one in which they can now SEE themselves, and if you can SEE it in your mind...you can make it reality.

You really must have a positive and sometimes even jovial personality, to be good at sales. Who do you think YOU would rather buy something from, a soothing voice on the phone, or a smiling face and a sincere handshake? Or buy from someone with a high pitched nervous voice or a shifty eyed fidgety person who can't look you in the eye?

With every word or gesture you cause your client/customer to either be drawn TO you, or repelled FROM you, either in very subtle almost unnoticed ways or more easy to understand ways, like...NO!

YOU ARE THE ARTIST

You paint the picture for your client/customer that you want them to see, hear, feel, and smell. You are the artist before the canvas of their imagination! Use this canvas in a way that before you are through painting, these people have already made the decision to buy, and can't wait to tell you they want it! Now all you have to do is just get out of their way and let them pay for it.

Did you ever know of a great artist that could create a great painting in an instant? Of course not, and neither can you paint a pleasing picture with them in it in just a few minutes. It's all about creating a new and more positive reality for someone, and this someone already needs/wants/has to have it, or they wouldn't be calling you or standing in front of you. This book is going to give you new tools to use in creating this positive new reality for your client/customer. It will also give you an entire set of new tools to navigate life in a more efficient way, with less effort and greater success.

It's going to tell you how to recognize someone who never hears you when they look right at you, and someone who can't hear you *unless* they are almost on top of you.

It will teach you to know exactly when someone is accessing THEIR brain for info and which part is in control.

There are other books out there written by even the founders of NLP slanted toward the sales profession, but none that put it in such easy to understand, simple language that you can take out and use right now. Some of this may sound like a "Snake oil salesman" talking to you, but don't knock it until you've tried it...or USED it.

The hardest part of adopting new ideas is to USE them when you're outside of your "Comfort zone". When this happens and you use the new knowledge to get results...that's when you know you've LEARNED something.

LEARNING:
When knowledge AQUIRED is APPLIED to achieve NEW desired results.

Pills don't do you any good in the bottle and knowledge doesn't do you any good unless you EMPLOY it. The hardest part about learning something new is to EMPLOY it when the going gets rough, things begin to "Go south" or the sale begins to slip away.

The first thing people do is to go back to what seems comfortable, what "Always use to work". But it doesn't work, and you keep using it, and it still doesn't work, and it doesn't work again and again. Then you find someone who it works on, and you say, "See I told 'ya, it would work, what a great salesperson I am". Now you've made one sale all week, while the people using the methods in this book have made 5 or 6. YOU HAVE NOT LEARNED ANYTHING YET!

AXIOM OF NON-ACHEIVEMENT:
If you keep doing what you've always done, you're going to get what you've always got.

The reason you're reading this book is to LEARN something. If you acquire new knowledge that will change things for the positive for you, BUT, you don't use it, what good is it? So practice something you've never done before. GET OUT OF YOUR COMFORT ZONE!!! It's the only way you will ever EMPLOY the new information acquired.

Then you will be able to say, "WOW, I learned something."

So get out there and USE this stuff, it will scare the daylights out of you when it works!

And it WILL WORK!

JUST DO IT!

CHAPTER 2
WHAT YOU NEED TO MAKE A SALE

Sales is the most highly paid profession (per hour) in the world no matter what field you choose to sell in, that's if you're good. If not, you will starve! It is widely recognized that in every sales organization 90% of the sales are done by 10% of the salespeople.
Why is this?

- All the top salespeople get the "Good" leads?
- All the top salespeople get Pre-qualified customers?
- All the top salespeople know the Boss's first borne?
- All the top salespeople work harder/longer?
- All the top salespeople lie to enhance the product?

The answer to all the above questions is of course **NO!**

The 10% know and have an intrinsic ability to recognize buying signs, capitalize on them and not waste time with non-buyers. They also have attention to detail, and this transfers to managing their time and their data. Data such as the leads they have been given without letting anything fall through the "Cracks" in their sales environment.

What almost every top salesperson has, and shares with each other is a thing called *WORK ETHIC*, and we will explore that in a future chapter.

For right now in this chapter let's define the necessary things that should be present to insure closing a deal, getting a signature on the dotted line, and at the end of the day, putting deposits in your bank account.

There ARE customers who have already investigated your product, and know all about it, and may want it. That's great, but the people that you contact who already want to buy what you're selling are very few and far between. If you think you are going to make a living on these "Laydowns" as we say, stock up on canned tuna fish, because that's all you will be eating and are going be able to afford, until you realize that you need to change what you're doing.

So what do you do? You CREATE the interest, along with a sales environment that has the necessary parameters present to HELP insure a sale.

Creating interest where there is none is a super tough assignment, but if there is just a seed of interest, this can be turned in to tall "Oak tree" of buyer obsession. You just need to point out some of the advantages of the product that may be little known, or stuck on the back page of the owner's manual. People don't really know how much they will like your product/service unless you tell them in a way that makes it sound like they can't figure out why they don't already HAVE it, and you are answering a question that was on their mind, but not yet asked.

You can say, "Most people ask me the question...xxxxx and here's the answer to that." Now you get to point out SEVERAL advantages in a manner that glorifies the product like the "Holy Grail", and soon they're asking how much it costs, when before they didn't even know they wanted it. To provide a "Fertile" ground for this budding desire you need three things and here they are.

3 THINGS NECESSARY FOR A SALE

A well known study of buyers' habits found after an exhaustive research, talking to many salespeople, and boiling it all down, the three things necessary for a sale are:

MONEY - **INTEREST**, and **CONTROL** (of the sales situation).

MONEY

JD Powers came out with a study of why people do not buy when confronted with the closing attempt, and they said the chief reason was: THEY DON'T HAVE THE MONEY!

If someone does not have the money it doesn't matter how much they want it, need it, GOT to have it, there will be NO SALE! The trouble is, they never want *you* to know they don't have the money, because that would make them look "Poor" and lowly. No one wants to look poor and lowly, and doesn't like being shown up as poor and lowly, so they act like they have the money and waste your time.

It is the salesperson's job to find out (really and truly) if they don't have the money, BEFORE spending 30 minutes, 10 minutes, or even 5 minutes on them. However; 9 out 10 people will tell you they DO have the money. So how do you find out? You talk to them, about anything ***but*** the product you're selling.

Find out ABOUT them, and the best way to do this is to ASK QUESTIONS.

After you ask a question, you do something very few salespeople (especially NEW sales people) do, which is...**LISTEN.**

When you say, "So John, what to you do for fun when you're not working, oh by the way what *do* you do?" Since people love to talk about themselves, they will begin to tell you things about themselves that you don't really need, or want to know, but keep LISTENING, because they will give you all the answers you are looking for to be able to sell the proverbial "Wet matches in a hurricane" to this person.

PROVERB:
GOOD SALESPEOPLE ARE GREAT TALKERS, GREAT SALESPEOPLE ARE GOOD LISTENERS.

Be careful at picking up the smaller details about someone, this gives you "Ammunition" for the sales situation that can make the difference between "Sale" and "No sale". For instance, just by listening or asking a few questions, (what kind of car do you drive, where do you work) you find out that they are working for minimum wage, don't own a car, and living with their parents.

Does this sound like a person that has extra money to give you? It should send up a red flag and make you doubt the credibility of them saying that they have $25,000 to invest in the IPO you're pushing. This is known as a ... TIME WASTER!

TIME WASTERS

Sometimes people just want someone to talk to, and strange as it seems, when you call them they've got nothing better to do but waste your time, and never buy anything. On the other hand they are very skilled at making you THINK they want to buy what you're selling, otherwise you'd hang up and then they would have to go back to petting their cat, polishing the silverware or whatever.

Sometimes it's a contest between them and you to see how long they can keep you on the line before YOU hang up. The quicker you can identify this type person the quicker you can move on to finding a better qualified customer.

SPOTTING A TIME WASTER

There are several "Red flags" that time wasters

always wave in front of you. The trouble is, many newbie salespeople never pick up on them, even when they are hit on the head with one. They figure, "If this person doesn't' hang up on me I'm doing great!" WRONG! It's your job to perceive a time waster in the first 3 minutes and get rid of them as fast as possible, because to you, TIME IS MONEY! Here are some examples of time wasters:

SUBJECT JUMPER*:*
You are explaining the product or advantage of it, and they start talking about something entirely different. Like, you say, "I'll stake my reputation on the fact that this product will do the job for you". They say, "Steak, I just had the worst steak in my life at this new truck stop down the road, there was so much fat on it that blah blah etc.....This person may have a mental impairment, or just was not listening to a word you said. If you get one of these people, either hang up or say you're going to the bathroom.
A study done at the University of Texas found that people remember: **20% percent of what they hear, and that's when they are LISTENING!**

If they do not listen...HANG UP, or excuse yourself.

PERSONAL PROBLEMS:
They've got to tell you about their daughter's, friend's mailman, or something equally unrelated. If it SEEMS boring or even if it seems interesting, either one, they are wasting your time because they *are not following you*. Bring them back with a phrase like, "So Bill, can you see yourself

picking this xxx up today so you can use it tomorrow?" This usually puts an end to the story telling and lets them know, it's BUY or Goodbye!
PROBING YOU:
They want to know *your* political views, and other personal issues. Don't get trapped into talking about yourself, which some newbies get hooked on, feeling this is a way to achieve "Rapport" with the client/customer, and later get a deal. In the end they say to call them back at a later date, and never ever buy, anything, EVER. - HANG UP!

HEALTH ISSUES
They want to tell you about their operation and all the pills they are taking. This could go on for a day or more. HANG UP! The minute someone gets off the subject of why you called, either get them back on or HANG UP!

It's your job as a "Green Beret" of sales to know after 3 minutes, "Is this person have a real potential for buying, or not." But, we'll go into that area later, which is, "To Pitch or Not to Pitch."

So after discovering some information about where the money is going to come from to buy what you're selling, what's next?

INTEREST

Most people who have plenty of money to buy are very skeptical of product claims, slippery salesman who promise everything but never deliver, and these people always want to know

about a "Return policy." If someone does not have the interest it doesn't matter if they have the money, there will be NO SALE! So, how do you find out if they have the interest?
Simple; ASK THEM! When they answer, listen to the TONE of their voice, the volume of their voice, and how well they make a statement without stuttering or stammering.

If they volunteer the information related to their interest or the LEVEL of their interest, this is a very good sign. Now is your chance to get them to talk about their interest. In every conversation there is a level of information IN BETWEEN the lines of what they say. This is where the closer type salesperson picks up valuable information to use later in developing greater interest.

Once again, you are in LISTENING mode!

Here is a great "Rule of thumb". As a person speaks, every 10 to 20 words in their sentence SHOULD tell you something about that person, IF you are listening close enough, with the idea, "What can I learn from each line." Make this your goal when talking to people, even people who you are not trying to sell something. This is great practice for you to be able to develop your listen skills. One great ability for you to develop is to REMEMBER THEIR NAME. This shows the person you are attuned to them, who they are and at least CARE enough to remember the small details about them. Plus, it's very embarrassing to have to ask them "Oh by the way, what did you say your name was."

If they talk about their private life, their family, how many kids, grandkids they have, they are indirectly telling you their age, (if on the phone and not in person), and if they are now or were married, may have put kids through college, have savings, IRA, pension, possibly retired, and may have some ready cash. Or, if they have a LOT of kids they may NOT have any money. But all of it is *information* about them so get as much of it as possible. Now is the chance for you to get them to talk more ABOUT themselves, and what they want from your service or product. This is where you REALLY learn if they are a buyer or NOT a buyer.

POLITICS

If they mention their political views, they are telling you which "Side" they are on as far as Dem or Rep, which can be very valuable on gaining rapport or losing rapport. Try to stay away from politics; it can only get you into trouble. There is no right answer for their political questions.

You need to be a "Sherlock Holmes" with a detective's mind, and ability to pick up "Clues" about what a person is thinking, or WILL think about what you say and HOW you say it. One wrong word can be like a "Bear trap" of a mistake in making someone feel comfortable, and in turn causing them to want to buy from you.

One wrong jab against the wrong political party/person can change the climate of the sales situation 180 degrees, ending in NO SALE. There is a 95% chance that being of the same political party, WILL NOT make the difference of getting a sale, and a 50/50 chance that saying the wrong thing about their favorite so and so, will be a deal breaker. There is a huge chance that if you are connected with the *opposing* political persuasion and or convictions, you will LOSE your the sale. Customers DO NOT BUY from someone they DO NOT LIKE. They just say they want to "Think about it first." Stay away from that area of conversation. Be neutral and get a sale.

You will find that sometimes that there is no good reason (or it's the strangest reason) why people buy something, and sometime it has nothing to do with WHAT is being bought, or the PRICE they will pay for it. A person will buy 3 quarts of ketchup from a membership warehouse, when they ALREADY have 2 quarts of it sitting in the pantry. Their reasoning: "You never know when you're going to need it in an "Emergency". They don't need it, they KNOW they don't need it, but "It's ON SALE!" "Think of the money we're saving", is the thought going through their heads. There's the story about the old lady who when she saw that cat food was 50% off for one day, bought 4 bags to cash in on the savings. Next day she bought a cat!

It's true they may need it or something like it, but many times it comes down to, "I just really liked that salesperson. They made me feel good about the product, the price, but mostly about MYSELF."

I've got a life long buddie that sells Mercedes Benz's. He makes more money than God! He told me that he's got a "Client/customer/now a friend, that he sold a car to (a long time ago), that comes by in the morning just to sit and have coffee and chew the fat with him. The notable thing is, he's bought 7 cars from him in 2 years, for himself, his wife, his kids, his son-in-law, and who knows. This guy just needs a friend to talk to, and he probably feels guilty by taking up so much of his time, that he buys a car every other month just to make it "Worth his while" to sit there and share some good times and conversation. But, before my friend KNEW he was loaded, he treated him with the same respect, and consideration anyone deserves by just being themselves, and wanting the best deal they can get on a car. Since my friend is just a naturally friendly guy, it was easy to make a new friend. That's why he's always one of, if not THE top salesman in the dealership.

SALEPERSON'S TRUTH:
People buy from people they LIKE. They don't like "Ass kissers", weak people who beg for a sale, and they don't like "Truth stretchers" and fibbers. Their main truth in the back of their head is, "Give it to me straight with no BS", if you adopt this philosophy you...will...make...money!

In creating interest, you've got to be able to allow; and the key word here is ALLOW, people to feel good about not only the product, but themselves, and THAT'S where the sale is really made, long before you ask for the signature on the dotted line. So...MAKE'EM FEEL GOOD!

CONTROL

If you cannot control the person (get info from them, get them to talk to you, open up a little) there will be NO SALE!

When you ask them a question about what they are looking for, or trying to accomplish with your product, investment, or why they need it, and they don't go along with answering this simple type of question, there is no control.

If you are selling an investment and you ask your potential client, "Where would the money come from Bill, your IRA, savings or would you have to move things around a bit?" If his answer is, "It's none of your business where it would come from", do you think he's going to give you $25,000 or is going to give you a credit card number over the phone? No control, = no sale!

If you say, "I'm sorry I can't hear you with the T.V. on so loud, would you mind turning it down a little?", and they say, "Sorry, I really want 'ta watch this" HANG UP, or walk out. They've just demonstrated to you that something is more important that you, or what you're selling, and also that they are pretty much set in their ways and you're not going to change this.

MOST IMPORTANT VARIABLE

Concerning the above variables, probably the most important I truly believe is the INTEREST factor. You can't change the money part, and you can't change the CONTROL part, but you *can* change the INTEREST factor.

You CAN cause an interest in your product or service with just a little effort on your part. That's the difference between an order taker and a master closer.

Now this is not a "Silver bullet" kind of secret magic wand effect. What this book is designed to do is to give you an edge in creating this level of interest where there was very little or sometimes actually no interest at all. THAT'S what sells product, and THAT'S what separates the order takers from the master closers.

So, if you think you're a salesman now, you're probably right, you make a good living doing what you're doing, selling what you're selling and you will go on doing it just like you're doing it now.

But...what if there was another part of selling that you were not aware of, another part of creating interest that you didn't even know existed. What if there was another world of master control and power control that you could exercise that would give you an additional edge? Would you be willing to take a look, give a listen, and see how it felt?

That's what we want to explore with this book, is giving you the "Forbidden knowledge" that most sales people never ever actually grasp, even though they somehow glimpse moments of greatness. Sometimes they always ask themselves, "What happened to the deal I was about to close, how did the client change into such a monster?" Or when they DO get a sale they say, "I never thought they (the client) would buy this." Which means when they actually do something right, they don't really know what it is, and can't duplicate it.

How do you do what you do when you do it perfectly, so you can create it again and again? That's what we want to focus on in the coming pages.

Every great sales person does certain things effectively, and other things not as good. We want to get you to put it all together to create the "Key" to each client's lock. This is the lock that keeps guarding their final decision, "OK you got me, let's do it", statement.

In this book you will find all kinds of concepts, some you are aware of and most likely some you are not aware of. These are things that you actually do now to bring about the "OK let's do it"; signal, but this will teach you how to re-learn this technique, to bring it to bear whenever you want to, at just the right time, to get just the right response.

This book is not just about teaching you how to sell, you may already know how to do that, if you are really new at it, then it's definitely for you.

ADEPTABILITY

If you are the experienced closer, it's about how to sell to people that you HATE to talk to, people that you don't like to sell to, and to close deals on people that you would normally want to "Blow off", after the first 30 seconds. How to "Change someone's mind", in a way that makes them think it's THEIR idea, and they are "Putting one over on YOU".

The REAL closers are the ones that are ADAPTABLE to the situation at hand and to the person in front of them or on the phone at the time. They are the people that are able to transcend the momentary frustration of the deal and client, NOT going their way and adapting to that client's desires, to MAKE it go their way. When you can do that, and KNOW you're doing it...WHILE you're doing it...then you're a MASTER CLOSER!

That's why this book is not only relevant to you, but will become your "Holy grail" of selling, and turn you into that Master Closer that is responsible for 90% of the sales in your organization or business.

You don't need to forget everything you know about selling, rearrange your techniques, re-think your strategies, and revamp your overall thinking.

You just need to see things in a different light, make a few changes and keep an open mind. The first time you put new knowledge into practice, and it works, you'll never be the same salesperson again.

CHAPTER 3
PRINCIPALS OF SUCCESSFUL SELLING

There have been several polls taken by major research firms in relation to self-education and a person's desire to better themselves in their chosen field. Through this research we find that salespeople are on the bottom rung of the ladder when it comes to keeping up on sales techniques and new developments that will give them an edge on successful selling. It turns out the 85% of salespeople currently making their living in sales for at least 3 years in this field, have never even read 1 book on sales training, or taken any advanced sales training in addition to the training they were given when starting their present job.

THE CONCEPT OF SELLING

Any kind of selling inevitably boils down to two basic rules. Product presentation and asking for the money, and asking for it seems to be the hardest part of the job for a lot of us.

The very best salespeople will argue that to be a successful salesperson you must practice the ABCs of selling, "Always Be Closing", but you need to PREPARE the customer for the close. If you've built a good relationship, discovered the customer's needs, gained a decent level of rapport, and advocated the right product, you have every reason to be confidant the customer will buy from you. Use that confidence to get the "YES" response from the customer, and you'll never go hungry.

It's called "ASSUMING" the sale. You ask questions that ASSUME the client/customer WILL be buying, or signing up to take the product/service. With this attitude and persona you transfer confidence, and a command personality to your customer/client, and they want to be counseled, led, and then SOLD, in that order.

When you consider the phrase, "Nothing is ever BOUGHT, it is SOLD", you begin to realize why the manufacturer of goods hires a salesperson to do one thing...SELL! They would love to get along without salespeople, they're hardheaded, long winded, talk too much, never satisfied, and not to mention, want to get paid, and paid too much (according to every boss that signs their check).

However; there is a reason that the boss keeps them around, MONEY! Even with paying their commission, the company makes more money than they would if they just put the product on the sidewalk and let people put the money in a can and take one.

There's another reason they are still around, there's very few good ones, that do their job, don't' gripe TOO much, and keep doing it day in and day out. That's called being a "Pro", and there are very few pros out there, and thank God for the newbies, because they make us look good, or at least better that we really are! There's one thing that a pro has that they don't give you in "Salesman's school", and that's...

CONFIDENCE

There is no substitute for confidence in sales. You MUST be confident when you ask for the sale, not overbearing "In your face" confidence, just the quiet self-confidence of someone has that says they don't have to prove anything to anybody, and they have proved it just by being who they really are. It makes the client/customer feel like you have been honest with them, not withheld information, and they can bank on everything you have told them. You SOUND like you know what you're talking about, you ACT like you know what they need, and you LOOK like someone who is forthright and honest. You would be surprised to know how many salespeople do not meet any, or least of all, every one of the parameters just mentioned.

The customer expects it, they can sense it, and when you display this level of confidence, it makes them feel like they have made the right decision by saying yes to your sales proposal.

BUILDING CONFIDENCE

How do you build confidence from the first time you pitch someone, or the first time you present your opportunity to a new client/customer?

The first element of building confidence is, know your product/service inside out. This means knowing all the answers to all the questions your client/customer has the possibility of asking. Some salespeople not only do NOT know the answers to these questions, they don't even know the *questions*.

Make sure you receive adequate training, and have all the rebuttals to all those questions BEFORE you hit the floor, the field, or the phone. THEN you will be confident, then you will make sales, THEN they will ask you to be the sales manger. (See chapter near the end)

You never have a second chance to make a first impression and once you give someone incorrect or bad information you're branded as a "Dummy" or "Untrustworthy", and that is almost impossible to reverse. Sometimes it it's almost impossible to know ALL the answers, so when you do get a stickler of a question you are not familiar with, don't try to "Come up" with an answer, or manufacture a "Probable" answer, just say "I don't know for sure on that, but I WILL find out for you." This insures two things, one is that your credibility remains in tact and two, and that you are honest enough to not BS someone with what they will eventually find out IS a fabrication of an answer and not actually the truth or the whole truth. Half the time they already know the answer to this question and they are just testing you to see what you do when you don't actually know the full correct answer to their question.

It's a funny thing about truth. It is like a big bubble under water, it ALWAYS comes to the surface, and you can't disguise it as something else BUT the truth. If you poke it under the surface it turns into 2 bubbles that you've got to handle and it gets worse from there on.

Once you know the truth, you WILL have confidence, and again, there is no substitute for confidence. REPEAT THAT 10 TIMES...RIGHT NOW! THERE IS NO SUBSITIUTE FOR CONFIDENCE... JUST DO IT!

CLOSING THE DEAL

We could write an entire book about the art of closing, and as you will learn in the chapters ahead. If you have done a good job of preparing the client/customer in gaining rapport and presentation, closing will be the easiest part of the deal.

You just need to know **when** to go for the close. Many say "early and often", but the best time is when the customer sends either verbal or nonverbal buying signals that they're ready to make their final purchasing decision. Some buying signals are obvious, and some are not so obvious signs, or ways the customer communicates that they are now ready to discuss making a purchase.

These signals usually take on the form of statements of need, desire, or questions about the product, from the customer, or they can be displayed in the customer's nonverbal body language. An example would be a greater attention to a specific area of the product/service, a fixed gaze or greater opening of the eyes in the direction of the product, or anything to display attraction to the product/service. Questions asking about the return policy of the establishment, and what kind of technical support, or post training you may offer. These are things that someone considers when they have gotten to the place of "Yes I'll take it" in their mind.

To a salesperson, these signals should be like a flashing red light and indicate the willingness and also readiness, to buy the product or service. If ***NOT*** capitalized upon, these signals CAN turn the buyer into a NON-buyer. When the salesperson misses or ignores these buying signals it's like telling the client/customer "I'm not really noticing your wants and or needs, I don't really care that much about you", and rapport is lost, possibly along with the sale. Bottom line: BE ATTENTIVE so you never miss the opportunity to say, "OK, let's write it up", and then DO IT!

LISTENING

Did you ever meet a salesman or saleswoman outside of their job, who didn't run off at the mouth constantly about every thought that came into their head? You can't get a word in edgewise, they don't even take a breath in between sentences, and you along with anyone involved in the conversation starts looking at their watch. This is the amateur salesperson that gives all salespeople a bad name and makes people say, "You must be in sales." They never listen to anything anyone says, and if they do it's only the sound of their talking to determine when there will be a break in their dialogue so THEY can start up again.

This is more of a personality trait sometimes, but it is much more common with people in sales, but we will go into listening in much greater detail later, because it is one trait that will make you more money with less effort, than anything you can do.

QUALIFICATION

One of the most important factors of successful selling is a little thing we call qualification. By this we mean you need to qualify the person you're trying to sell as to having all or most of the main things necessary to complete the sale. To recap, do they have the money, do they have the interest, and are they controllable?

MAKE A FRIEND MAKE A SALE?

Someone said, "Make a friend, make a sale", that's a good idea, but don't go over board. There is nothing wrong with being friendly, just not their BEST friend. People can say no to their friend easier that to a command personality, with a firm attitude of a leader. Be cordial, courteous, and informative, and they will perceive you and someone they would like to know, not so much as a "Good buddy". This may make the difference between "I'll have to think about it", and "Let's do it."

CUSTOMER SATISFACTION

A satisfied customer or client defined is very simple, they are pleased with what they got, what they got was what they thought they were getting, and in the end they're happy. That's fairly easy to create in a client/customer, right? If it's so easy, why are there not more satisfied customers out there who have said, "Yes" to a salesperson? Let's examine why so many may people are DISSATIFIED with their product or service after they receive it.

It was not as the salesperson described. It didn't not do what it was suppose to do, or did it poorly. Research has found this is the most repeated reason for customer dissatisfaction. They simply didn't get what they ordered, bought, or THOUGHT they bought.

DEFFINITON: Good salesperson - Someone who can make his/her product or service appear better than the competition WITHOUT LIEING.

So many sales people (especially phone salespeople) are inclined to inflate claims, butter the bread on both sides, lay it on a little thick, and forget to mention things that would turn someone off, or make them "Want to think about it".

This causes both sides of the sales situation (customer and salesperson) a cascading deluge of problems that just keep getting worse. It ends up with the client or customer not only being dissatisfied, but spreading "Bad press", and energy all over this known Universe. They tell everyone about how poorly they were treated, and what a rotten, no good, low down company they had to deal with along with who the salesperson was that caused it all. In your dealings with people you have to ask yourself, do you want to be as truthful as you can, and not raise these kinds of problems, or do you just want to skate by, taking the easy way, inflating claims, telling little white lies, and collecting your commission? When you do these kinds of things you create an axe over your head that's just waiting to come crashing down on your neck when you least expect it to happen, and it WILL happen! DON'T DO IT

THINGS NEEDED FOR A SALE
THE "BIG 3" AS PREVIOUSLY STATED

1. Money – No money = no sale.
JD Powers did a survey, and said lack of funds was #1 reason for potential clients not buying when confronted with the closing attempt at a sale. So, how do you find out if the person has the money? The first thing to do would be to ASK THEM! Trouble is, if you ask too soon before you build up the benefits of the product or service you will get a cold reception, and the answer will most likely be "I don't give that info out." Very few people go to a car lot intending to buy a car THAT DAY. They're all "Just looking". They never really become serious until they sit in the driver's seat, smell that new car smell, begin to realize all the special features as the salesman points them out, and then when they hear the price it's justified. Price quotation without justification = no sale! They will all tell you they have the money; nobody likes to appear poor, without funds,

destitute, or a loser. So it's up to you to be able to read between the lines of conversation and use your powers of deduction when testing them for available funds. Never forget the statement: *Price quotation without justification = no sale.*

2. Interest - There must be *some* degree of interest to motivate the buyer or your job will be to CREATE the interest. Now if a person has absolutely NO interest in your product, why would they be in your sphere of influence? So just by the fact that you are talking to them, especially in person, says there is SOME degree of interest. Exceptions would be if you are in a telemarketing room on a predictive dialer or press one campaign where random numbers are dialed to people who just barely fit the parameters of need.

So now it's up to you to cultivate the interest no matter how slight, and that is what we would like to focus on.

Creation of interest
Can a salesman CREATE the interest? It is easier to enhance the interest rather than create it from scratch, but it's not impossible.

Ask Questions
You need to find hot buttons, push them and see what you get for responses. These questions can also bring out a small amount of interest, and from there you can build on a foundation to create a greater interest. Sometimes people will become more interested in a product or service when they learn something they didn't already

know about the product. This knowledge leads to wanting to know more about the product or service, and the more they know, the better informed decision they can make about buying.

Questions are answers
This means you will learn more about someone by asking questions and letting them volunteer information than any other means. What do they do for a living, are they married, do they have children, where to they live, all this goes together to make a picture. In the end does the picture support their claim, "Sure I've got the money / credit rating", etc? When you ask them about the money, do they divulge that information readily or refuse to give you and answer? This is an indication of their "Controllability", which we'll get into later, but it's good to know as soon as you can.

3. Control - You must be able to control the sales situation, environment, and eventually the potential client.

Lack of YOUR control might result from:

- Language barrier – Cannot understand you
- Bad phone connection
- Buyer distraction - Screaming baby, dogs barking, doorbell etc.
- Strong personality - wants to be in control
- Too busy – Cannot talk when you call
- Irritated – Outside problems my distract
- Bad health – More pressing issues than buying what you're selling
- Friend/spouse – May be a distraction

NEVER WASTE TIME

In the sales business, time is truly money. When you get involved with useless conversation with a client or potential client, your time is being wasted, and the true "Sales professional" knows when the red light of USELESS VERBAGE begins to blink, and the bell begins to clang. They are quick to not only realize this, but also do something about it, change the conversation, terminate the call, or whatever they have to do to turn things around. Below are some "Get off the phone" or, "Don't waste your time", signals you should pick up immediately.

1. Not the decision maker
2. Just lost my job - no money
3. No credit card - may mean no money
4. Just renewed/bought it
5. Hostility - Won't listen to you
6. No English - Does not understand you
7. Bad connection - If on the phone
8. Talks over you - No control
9. Argumentative - Unreasonable
10. Know it all - Already made up their mind

IMPORTANCE OF RAPPORT

In order to have a good pre-sales experience you must gain rapport with the potential client. This means gaining their confidence, and respect. The more subjects you can talk about, the more common ground you can find between you and the client/customer, the faster and more quality rapport you will have with them.

WHAT IS RAPPORT?

When the client truly believes that you have their best interests at heart, you share the same interests, views, and are on the "Same page" as them with their ideas and beliefs. This is why asking questions and allowing them to talk about themselves as much as they want, will be an asset later. If you like the same sports, the same team, if you come from the same geographic area, anything that puts you both on common ground initiates that rapport between you both that will be of great help in the future.

GAINING RAPPORT

1. MIRRORING
Be just like, talk just like, act just like the person you are selling to. However they stand/sit, do the same, however they walk, do the same, the speed with which they talk, do the same. You want to be a "Mirror" to the person in front of you or on the phone.

2. MATCHING
You adopt their rate of speech, level of intensity, and speed of vocalization, you walk, talk, and make gestures just like them, you BECOME them.

3. PACING
Get THEM to come up to...or down to...your level of speech, in speed, volume and level.

THE CLOSE WITHOUT CLOSING

THE TIE DOWN

A tie-down is a way of making sure the client is "With you" in their level of understanding what the product/service is all about. Another reason for the tie-down, is that it tells you how much they may want or need it, and gives them a better idea of how it will benefit them. Also it shows them how they will use it, and in general lets YOU know if they are following you and your presentation AT ALL. On the same level, it will tell you how much information they have absorbed related to how much you have told them.

Very simply it "Ties them down" to what you THINK they should know, or be interested in, to produce a "Yes" at the close.

So many salespeople go on and on, talking (instead of listening) about the product or service, because they think that unloading a ton of information in the shortest amount of time is what will cause someone to want to buy something. WRONG! If you don't use the tie-down as a way of bringing your client/customer along with you on the journey of the little game called, "Presentation-question...Presentation-question", etc., then you should go back to being an order taker, or a fry cook, because you're going to STARVE as a salesperson!

You may be talking, talking, talking but they hear only about 20% of what you're saying as far as content retention. This is because they are thinking of how and if they will use the product or service you are pitching. If they are going to absorb what you are saying, they should *not* be thinking of something else at the same time if they are truly listening to what you are telling them. The tie-down is a way of letting YOU know if they are following what you are saying, understand what you just said and also their level of interest in the product and that exact moment.

I learned this in a very hard but lasting experience. I was selling FCC Specialized Mobil Radio Licenses, and talking to a farmer in Kentucky. For 5 minutes I was going on and on and on about how the purchase of this investment would net him thousands of dollars in a very short amount of time. I kept telling and telling and spouting figures and projections (he could have put the phone down and gone to the bathroom for all I knew). Finally I said, "So all we need is your check for the $3700 and we can get you into the program, I'll have FedEx come by tomorrow, to pick up your check, which is better morning or afternoon?"
His response:
DO WHAATTT NEIGHAUGHANOWWWW?

He had absolutely no idea of what I had just said for the last 10 minutes, or who I was, what I wanted or what I was talking about, because I never stopped to do a TIE DOWN in the first 30 seconds, or at any time in the presentation.

That is why we use tie-downs to keep the client/customer on the "Same page" as us, and keep them engaged in the "Education process". The Tie Down, lets them know why they should buy our product/service and how it will help them. Another thing it does, is keeps THEM in their own mind, tracking what you say, and aware of information that they may MISS. When they say, "Wait a minute, do what?" You get to clarify some information that may be ambiguous to them. And, all you need is a little ambiguous info in their mind to bring about the, "I need to think about it" response.

Some examples of a tie down would be:
1. Are you with me?
2. Wouldn't that be great?
3. Wouldn't you agree?
4. Everyone knows that, right?
5. Great idea, right?

TALKING TO A CAT

The best way I can illustrate the blah blah blah syndrome is that if you don't use tie-downs on your client/customers it's just like talking to a cat.

People who have a cat have gotten very close to their animal and they have this great misconception that when they talk to their cat it actually UNDERSTANDS them. Now cats are very affectionate, cuddly, and wonderful companions, but they DO NOT UNDERSTAND ENGLISH!
So...when Fluffy jumps up on the couch and you say, "No Fluffy, don't get up on the couch, your

claws will catch and pull the treads out of the couch pillows, and then I'll have to take it to the upholstery shop and pay a lot of money to get it repaired, now get down."
Fluffy's little head cocks to the side, and her eyes get all big and bright and she licks her whiskers...but there's NOTHING...going...in!
She knows when she hears, "Fluffy" she gets fed, or petted, so all she hears is, "Blah blah, yaaablah FLUFFY, blah"Blah blah, yaaablah FLUFFY, blah
"Blah blah, yaaablah FLUFFY, blah
"Blah blah, yaaablah FLUFFY, blah
"Blah blah, yaaablah FLUFFY, blah woo, kiss, hug and pet.

The same thing can happen to your client/customer if you don't use a few tie-downs to see if they are with you. All they hear is "Blah blah, yaaablah **$185.00**, blah, Blah blah, yaaablah **best product**, blahBlah blah, yaaa blah **do the job**, blah
Blah blah, yaaassss blah **on sale**, blah, and have no idea about anything you said specifically. In the end they will tell you what you've heard all day..."I'll have to think about it."

USE TIE-DOWNS! They're questions, ask questions or go back to your dishwasher job, you'll be more successful there!

DECISION MAKING AXIOM
It is much easier to GET a decision that to CHANGE one.
So what you need is a "Mini-Decision" in the positive area of thinking about the product or

service. This allows the client/customer to acknowledge that it will do the job intended, they do have a need for it, and that they agree with the positive statements or claims you have made about it, all WITHOUT committing to buying it right then. How do you get this "Mini-decision" from them? You use the TRIAL CLOSE.

THE TRIAL CLOSE

A trial close is just what it implies, a trial at closing the sale, but without a serious risk of making someone feel "Penned in" or uncomfortable. You get them to admit their need, confirm a positive aspect or claim about the product, and in general to AGREE with you about something...anything. This may be the first "Yes" you get from the client/customer, and of course you want them to get into the habit of saying this word, "YES", as many times as you can, as often as you can and whenever you can.

A trial close is supposed to take someone's "Temperature" as it relates to their desire to acquire the product or service being pitched. It is a very wise technique that the better closers use to give them an indication of how close the client/customer is to saying "Yes" to the actual closing question when it IS presented.
It can be in the form of a probing question to find the level of need, desire, and emotional attachment the prospect has to the product or service. It is good if you can work it into the conversation using THEIR words or phrases. That's why it is so important to be, as stated in

this book, a "Good listener"! When they something to declare their level of approval on a certain aspect of the product or service you are trying to sell, you need to pick up on this little quip or quirk instantly. You can follow it up with something like, "I'm glad you mentioned that aspect of our service", or "I can see you've done your homework here, and I think you'll love the way we've handled the xxxxx portion of xxxx.
Without a trial close you have very little idea of where the client/customer is coming from as far as their level of seriousness in making the actual purchase.
Some examples would be:
1. Would this be about the right size for your xxx, and would the color go with your xxx?
2. What do you think your xxx (wife, husband, girlfriend etc.) would think about the xxxx?
3. Would you like us to cart away your old xxx, we would do that for free?
4. Have you ever had one of these xxx before?
A more leading or stronger trial close would be a closing question that will indirectly implicate them as saying yes to the sale no matter how they answer. "Are you still at Xxx Street so I can get your free gifts out to you right away, as a way of saying thanks?"

"Which would you like to use for payment, Visa or Master card?"
This is your first attempt at testing their level of interest. Usually the answer is something like, "Whoa now, wait a minute here, I never said I was gon'a buy anything." This tells you about how *controllable* a potential client is, and gives you an

indication of how close they are to saying, "Yes" to the sale. Instant resistance tells you to go slower, and non-resistance tells you keep closing.

Other good trial closes are, "So which one seems it would be the best choice for you, number 1 or number 2?" No matter which one they pick, they are saying yes to the sale.
NEVER EVER *EVER*...ask if they would like to "Take advantage of this sale now", it's too closed ended, THEY would be admitting to the sale directly, they never want to say YES to a salesman, they're conditioned to always say NO or I need to think about it etc. When you ask "If they "Want to take advantage" of this etc., you're asking THEM to close the sale, do you really think they're going to close themselves? If this were the case we wouldn't need salesmen at all, just put the product out there with a phone number, and then just take orders.

People never like to be finally asked the question that will commit them to the sale. They know it's coming, they know they are going to have to say yes, or no, and if it's no, they are going to have to find a reason to justify it, and a whole lot of other mental gyrations that their mind is already dong at that time.

So, the use of the trial close is very powerful in revealing EARLY in the sales process just what those objections are so they can be dealt with *before* the end of the sales presentation. Then when the final closing question is asked, if the salesperson has done their job effectively, the client will be "Boxed in" with nowhere to go except to say, "Yes", or look/seem really foolish for saying "No".

Since not all buying signals guarantee immediate closure, it is important that when you identify one or more of these buying signals that you use the trial close AT THAT TIME.
Remember, the secret to closing is not how to ask it, but WHEN to ask it. Many salespeople are afraid to ask for the sale in fear they may be rejected. There's a reason for this. If a customer rejects you before they are ready to buy, it reduces your confidence, while putting you in a position to change the customer's mind.

The important point to take home about the trial close is that you're not asking for a decision. A trial close asks for an OPINION and not for a decision. The trial close is designed to answer the question, "When is it appropriate to ask for the sale?" Some have called it the salesperson's "Temperature taker", since it is used to measure the customer's temperature towards making their purchase. But the trial close serves a dual purpose. Top salespeople, not only use this technique to check the customer's willingness to buy, but to gauge the match of their customer towards the product being presented.

In other words you're trying to see how the customer "feels" towards a specific product. The more positive responses you can receive from a customer, the more likely you will be able to ask for the sale, and know ***when*** to do so. If you receive a "cold" response, it may mean you have to change the presentation to a different product/service or level of presentation, but at any rate you are on the wrong product, service, or level of presentation. This is very important to know as early as possible so you can deal with it as early as possible. If a "NO" is in the back of the client/customer's mind in the beginning of the presentation, it WILL come to the surface sooner or later, and most of the time at the moment of the close. The main focus here is to bring out the negative idea, complaint, or excuse as early as possible, so it can be dealt with a.s.a.p.

Remember, trial closing is not asking for the sale, but merely asking the customer's opinion and preparing them for the sale. This is an important difference to keep in mind.

There are three key concepts to keep in mind as you're developing trial close questions or statements:

1. A trial close does NOT ask for the sale.
For instance, a trial close question may be: "After seeing this new feature on our state of the art machine, isn't it amazing how it can make your job so much easier"?

The direct close, which asks for a decision, would sound like:
"I can have this product delivered to your house tomorrow. May I put that on your charge card or would you like to just pay cash?"

Notice in the *trial* close, you are not causing them to make a yes or no decision on buying and do not have the risk of a "no" response from the customer.

Without that risk, there is little potential for losing the sale. While in the direct close, if you attempt to ask for the sale too early, the customer's "no" response will put them in a role of defending their decision. There's a saying in selling, "It's much easier to **get** a decision than to **change** one", and therefore once a customer has voiced that decision...it's very difficult to persuade them otherwise.

2. A trial close should purposely assume that the customer intends to purchase the item.
For instance, use phrases like "When we deliver", or "Will you need a XXX for your new XXX?" These type phrases will encourage the customer to move from debating the purchase to making the buying decision. If you have asked the right questions in which the customer assumes ownership and the customer's response has been positive, then the next logical step would be to ask for the sale.

3. A trial close should always produce a positive response from the customer.
Although you will not always receive a positive customer response, trial closes should always be attempted when the customer has displayed positive buying signals towards a product. If the customer has not demonstrated these buying

signals it may not be the ideal time to use a trial close, and could even be detrimental.

In the discovery phase of the selling process, we preach never to ask closed ended questions. On the other hand, in the trial close stage this can be used to your advantage.

Questions like, "Do you like this color?" "Do you need your old product hauled away? Or "Would you like me to show you how to operate this XXX?", if asked when the customer is demonstrating various buying signals, you should get a "yes" from the customer. The more "yes" responses the customer gives you, the more likely they will say "yes" when it comes time to make their buying decision.

Most salespeople would believe that trial closes should occur towards the end of their sales presentation, but that's far from the actual truth. It's often worthwhile to do several trial closes throughout the entire selling process.

The best solution is to trial close "early and often" and while doing so, as with most closes, be quiet, watching and listening carefully for their response. Sometimes the customer's reaction to the trial close may be so positive; it will lead you right into asking for the sale at that time.

Failure to trial close often, also may delay the actual close, which could have a similar effect such as asking for the sale too early. In this case, you've missed the customer's peak desire to make the purchase and instead of agreeing to a decision, the customer is more likely to stall and make excuses on why they should not buy your product.

Never be afraid of finding out what your customer is thinking and feeling. When you use trial closes, you will successfully set up the customer for the sale and dramatically increase your chances that you will be able to move to the next logical step, which is asking for it!

4. Below are some trial closes you can try.

A. Will you need your old xxx hauled away?
B. How do you think that our new XXX color would look in your xxx room?
C. We have a 12 month no interest, no payment offer, how do you FEEL about that?
D. Would your new XXX be going upstairs?
E. Do you like the idea of never changing a xxx on your new xxx?
F. What do you like best about this new product?
G. Do you feel this xxx will be able to do the job you want?
H. Won't the big game look great on this new xxx cable?

The way a customer answers questions like these should give you a clear idea of what they're thinking. If you feel the customer is positive and comfortable, it's time to close the sale. If you feel they're not, you might want to revisit the info gathering or/discovery phase to gather more information about the customer's needs and wants.

INFORMATION GATHERING AND CATCHING THE FISH

ALLOW the client to tell you about their experiences, give them some audio space, and they will tell you what is important to them. Is it time, money, security, advancement, growth, mutual funds, whatever. It's like catching a big fish on a light line, you just can't jerk it in, too much pressure all at once and the line (or client) snaps, and they're gone.
They have to be "Played with a gentle hand". Once again...ASK QUESTIONS and LISTEN, more than you talk.

The client has a series of "Locks" that you must get the "Keys" to, and then only by the use of the ***right key*** in the ***right lock***, used at the ***right time*** - will get you the answer for which you are searching. Which is what motivates them, and drives them to have an interest, no matter how slight, in what you're selling.

After you have a reasonable idea of these interests, desires, and drives, then you can begin to design and shape your pitch or sales strategy to fit your potential client/customer just like the key mentioned earlier.

In the end if you've designed the right "Key" the lock will pop open and you'll hear, I'll take it", or "Here's the card number" or "Oh well, we may as well get it now."

CHAPTER 4
OBJECTIONS & HANDLING THEM

Somebody who was a great sales trainer once said, "Your job doesn't start until the customer says NO". Doesn't that sum up the "Closer's" job? In every sales situation the potential client/customer is NEVER convinced that YOUR opportunity or product is the best one for them. That's when your job actually begins. If you as a sales person had to hang on "Laydowns" (people who will just say "Yes" to your closing attempt), you would be classified as an "Order taker" and you would not have a commission structure befitting a CLOSER! A closer NEVER takes NO for an answer, and always has a rebuttal that sounds just like he or she never heard the objection that was given. That's why sales is the highest paid position in the company hierarchy of money paid for the amount of hours worked. It is because the top sales people have that gift of being able to take rejection, having doors slammed in their face and still come back to present the customer/client with yet an another alternative choice that results in a "Yes, I'll do it". These are the salespeople we call CLOSERS, and if you look at their life in general, they all fall into the same general slot or have the same basic profile. They drive one of the newest or nicest cars parked the company lot. They wear the most up to date fashion in clothing, and everyone seems to want to be "With" them because they're "Cool", or at least perceived that way. They have the best looking girl friend, or wife, if they're a guy, and husband boy friend if a

woman.
But all kidding aside, it can be best illustrated by the following scenario.

THE BUYER/SELLER GAME

The game works like this. The seller contacts all the people he or she thinks are good prospects for the product or service being sold. The first contact is usually by phone, if not 100% by phone. Then depending upon the resistance to the initial pitch or presentation, the salesman/woman then continues the pitch/presentation hoping the potential customer/client is still listening and not put the phone down and gone to the bathroom. If the salesperson is good they should throw out questions to see if anyone is still there, let alone listening or caring. After the presentation the salesperson attempts to close the deal and get payment, but of course there is a small glitch in the whole plan devised by the salesperson. The potential customer/client, wanting the best possible price on said product or services will always pretend a lack of interest, and feign lack of need in the product or service as an initial test of the salesperson's skill and ability to handle rejection. Sometimes this potential customer will actually tell the salesperson to call them back at another time, or walk out of the establishment, to enforce the pretense of low interest in the product or service. The buyer may also feel they can get a better deal or price, by employing these tactics. They know if they say NO enough times they WILL get a better price/deal, because they know how to play the "Buyer/Seller Game", and have won the game (they think) several times in the past. It is now the salesperson's opportunity to feign weakness with the "Broken wing" tactic, (pretending to be "New" at all this sales stuff, or lack of product knowledge) to make the client *"Think"* they are smarter, have superior knowledge, and more in control.

Once again this puts the customer/client at ease, and brings a new level of comfort to the customer/client, causing them to again lower their guard against the close that they think is come and gone.

THE "TAKE-AWAY"

It is at this time the salesperson will gently assert themselves in maintaining the standing price, (which is never set in stone) and to pretend to be so busy with other customers/clients that a call back is impossible, or that *when* they come back the product/service will not be available at that price/color/size etc. This is to give the outward appearance that they can do nothing to vary or lower the price, and have so many opportunities to sell the product that they are too busy to call back.
Once the customer/client TRULY believes that the price initially quoted in the "Special" discount is the locked in, can't change it, set in stone...price, then and only then will the salesperson drop the price.

The game continues...

The salesperson may even suggest that, "Maybe this product/service is not right for you." Depending upon how convincing they are the potential customer/client may begin to show signs of desire and need of the product or service. They may even let their guard down, thinking the act of the salesperson closing on them has gone by, and now they won't need an excuse for not buying at this time.

Now the salesperson interjects the possibility of a lower price predicated, of course, on checking with his boss, manager etc., to get special "Permission" to offer this price, making the customer feel equally special, and like they are getting this extra special/special ...deal not offered to just everyone. This interjection of price change puts a new spin on the sales situation, and makes the product/service look, and sound, much more appealing. While making the product or service seem more attractive, and now the salesperson slips in a trial close to test the "Temperature" of the client as it relates to YES or NO. Something like, "When we deliver your xxx would you like us to take your old xxx away, we would do that for free!"
Soon the customer is agreeing to the whole thing, because it just feels right, looks right, and sounds right. The best thing is, they THINK they've won "The Sales Game", and that's what you call a satisfied customer, and that's what you call a master closer.

But...back to objections and how to handle them without seeming to disagree or challenge the potential customer client. First of all, you can object to something with out being overly argumentative. The quickest way to loose rapport with a client/customer is having an argument with them.

AN ARGUMENT

So what constitutes an argument? The dictionary says an argument is: *A reason or set of reasons given with the aim of persuading others that an action or idea is right or wrong.*
So...the idea of persuading someone that their idea, event, perception, or whatever is WRONG, will be the beginning of an argument, that you will NEVER ever win.

FACT: NOBODY, ever, and I mean ever, "Wins" an argument. One person just walks away believing what they've always believed, the other does the same, with less degree of affinity (caring) for the other.

Even if you present more compelling, more concrete, and more "Correct" pieces of information, the other person, customer/client will walk away unconvinced of your point of view. They will also walk away...WITH THEIR MONEY STILL in their wallet, bank account, or still on their credit card. You may have out shined them in knowledge about xxx, or showed them where they were, "Wrong", but it still ended in a "NO SALE", making you the loser. You "Won the battle, but lost the war". How many people have you ever had say at the end of an argument, (who were not being sarcastic) "Ya know you were right and I was wrong?" There will always be people that have the idea, "I believe what I believe, so don't confuse me with the *FACTS!*" So you see, it doesn't matter what YOU think, or what YOU believe, all that matters is what the client/customer believes. If they believe that you have their best interest at heart, then that trumps everything else, and how can they do that if you're arguing with them, no matter who comes out on top.

FACT: Customers/clients buy from people they LIKE, and do not buy from people they do NOT LIKE. Real shocker huh?

So how do you present opposing views, facts, or information to someone who is giving you negative buying signs or resistance to being closed on a deal or product? You do it in a positive way rather that a negative way. Here are some examples:

NEGATIVE SLANTED PITCH:

You SHOULDN'T buy one of those xxx (competitor products) they'll only break down on you before you use them an hour etc. Only an IDIOT would buy one of those xxx.

POSITIVE: *Of all the products on the market I feel our xxx is very superior to xxx (competitor) because xxxx. The track record on repairs or xxx is so much better than xxxx. I think you'll be a lot happier with our xxx.*

NEGATIVE SLANTED PITCH: *Anyone knows how bad that xxx is when it comes to xxx. If you buy one of those you'll be very dissatisfied after the first month.*

In this instance you are slamming the competition, and people generally don't like to hear a lot of negative input about anything or anyone. That's why it's always a last resort in political campaigns, because is brings the negativity back to the accuser. You can't sling mud without getting dirt on your hands. You can mention how your product or service is more POSITIVE than the competition, will perform better, last longer, and is just superior in general. In stead of naming the actual competitor you can refer to them in general terms like, "Most of the other xxx companies or xxx manufacturers" may be lacking in xxx areas we discussed here today". Staying positive in all descriptions of your product or service as it relates to the competition, will get you a lot farther toward the close and a "Yes" from your client/customer, than running down the competition by finding fault with it.

POSITIVE:

When you compare our xxx with that product by xxx (competitor) you'll find that there are several advantages you might not see at first. In the end you'll really be glad you chose our xxx for your family or xxx.

You should always tailor your responses to a

customer/client's objections in a manner so as to highlight your product without trashing your competitor or "Mud slinging" so to speak. Use phrases like, "When you take a closer look at xxx, you see the difference is xxx" or, using the client/customer's own words..."Let's examine that fact you just mentioned" and always put a positive note on your product **AT THE END OF THE SENTENCE**. This leaves the client/customer with that positive fact to remember, and it sticks in their mind longer. This can make the difference between avoiding an argument and closing a sale. All references to competitor's products should be tempered with a neutral judgment being careful to keep negativity out of any thing you say, no matter which product/service you are referring to.

TYPES OF OBJECTIONS TO BUYING

HAVEN'T GOT THE MONEY

This is probably the most heard objection in sales. People think if YOU think they don't have the money you won't try to SELL them XXX or at worst CLOSE on them to buy XXX.

"I don't have the money" just means, "I don't want to SPEND the money...MY money, or THIS amount of money, on your product/service. It's either not worth it or I don't THINK it's worth it, and I'm not interested enough in to give you the money". People have to think that they are getting something that's worth more...much more than they are paying for it.

There is one exception to the rule, and that's the person who is buying something that just by the fact that they own it, says he or she spent a lot of money on it. Those things in that category would be yachts, airplanes, season tickets to xxx, a second cabin in the mountains, and the list is very clear.

So...unless you have one of those types of sales jobs (Selling Farris, Lear jets, or Rolls Royces) you better pay close attention to the pages of this book, because they will make you more money than waiting for one of those types of customers to walk through the door.

But for the average Joe, deciding on which washer/dryer to get, the money "Seems" to be the most repeated objection. So, your job is to find out what the ACTUAL reason/s are for in not taking advantage of your "Sale".

FACT: When somebody REALLY wants something, they WANT IT! Price is a hurdle they can jump if they find someone who can work with them.

YOUR RESPONSE:

1. If money were no longer a problem for you, would you choose xxx or yyy to take home/order/buy TODAY?

2. If I could take care of the money problem and throw that totally out the window, would you take it home with you today, mean if price were never an issue, would we have a deal?

You have to get the client/customer to the place of already POSSESSING the object, using it, getting benefit from it, enjoying it, then and only then will they cast off the attitude that they can't afford it. With your help (and financing) they can afford this product/service when they never thought they could before.

That's what changes pay checks, and lives. Your ability to take a situation that looks negative, and like it's going down for the last time...the sale is lost, and bringing it back up with the customer/client leaving happy, and feeling like he/she won in the price vs. quality battle. For all intents and purposes she WON! They get to tell all their friends how they talked this "Bug" of a salesperson into the deal of the century and them getting the best deal because of their negotiating skills. Now ANYONE wanting one of what you're selling is calling YOU! It's even worth it if you let one of them win once in a while and you the salesperson make very little or nothing. You can't buy that kind of good will, and positive advertising. When people come to you as referrals they always DO have the money, and this is way to build business. There are so many crooked sales people out there, that when someone meets, and does business with an honest person, it's like gold to them. Pretty soon you're in a network of "Gold" people, and you're making more money per hour that you ever were, all because you handled a few objections about a product from someone who never used it in the first place. You gave them a good deal; they were satisfied and told a lot of other people about how credible you were.

AND THEY DIDN'T HAVE THE MONEY!~~~

MY WIFE/HUSBAND/LAWYER WON'T LET ME BUY IT/DO IT

This is the classic "Blame it on someone else" tactic. They just tell you that the decision maker (which you can't talk to) is the reason for the NO SALE. This separates them from having to make a decision because the decision must be made by someone else, that's never available. Some people will or can never just say NO to a salesperson. They would rather come up with a "Reason" why they have to NOT buy what you're selling, and this is it. In your pre-sales interview if you asked the right questions this would not be an issue, because one of those questions should have been, *"Are you the only person who makes the decisions in your household"?* When they say they are that person, you continue to tell them that if there is another person need be involved, you can call back when ALL people are present, or to bring that person in before you give them any kind of a "Real competitive" price on the product/services.

FACT: Buyers are liars.

It sounds very cruel/callous, but sadly it's true. People will make up the most outrageous lies, fabrications, and stories to get out of telling a salesperson the true reason for not buying. They will always come up with some kind of reason why they have to put off a decision to buy, or feed you incorrect information about their ability to pay, be the decision maker, or what their true desire is in the type of product they are looking for. If they really love the color red in an auto, and they see one they like, they'll tell you how much they hate the color, but if it was a better price they "MIGHT" be able to "Learn to like it".

YOUR RESPONSE: (To "My spouse won't let me buy it")
First of all you agree with them that your spouse is just the same way, and that how you went ahead and made the decision to buy something right on the spot, that saved you BOTH A TON OF MONEY.

You tell them what a great surprise their spouse will get when they see how much money they BOTH have saved TODAY...by that person taking action and buying while the *sale was still on*. They can tell their spouse that they knew they would not get the chance at that price if they walked out the door or hung up the phone without buying.

You mention that you never knew any husband/wife who would get mad at a spouse that saved them "This kind of money."

Everyone who uses the "Spouse excuse" is just not satisfied with the positive reasons you've given them for buying the product or service, and need more convincing, or motivation. You need to dig a little further into their background and "Situation" to find what it is that will motivate them to trigger that buying signal in their brain. Finding this buying trigger is the key to the sale, because some people just plain and simple, have no buying trigger, and will always be "Lookie

Loues" and it's your purpose to find this out as quickly as possible so as not to waste a huge amount of time on them.

I NEED TO THINK ABOUT IT

This is THE most heard objection in the world of sales and always has been. It just means the person has not been convinced properly, or the needed level of rapport has not been achieved yet, or you haven't hit upon the exact reason that is preventing them from buying. It's up to you to find out what that reason or discrepancy *actually* is in reality. Then you can deal with the REAL objection.

EXAMPLE:
A guy comes into a marine supply store and is looking at an inflatable boat for sale. The salesman makes him a special price, he says no. Salesman asks him what he wants in a small boat, wants to fish, needs the exercise rowing, what ever. He says, "I'm just not sure if it's right for me. Salesman finally asks a few questions (as stated, very important task) says, "Have you ever had a boat like this before?" Guy says, no but my Father did when I was a kid, I fell out of it and darn near drowned." NOW we know what the problem is! This guy is afraid of water, and here's a salesman trying to figure out why he doesn't want this boat at such a special price! Instead of changing the price on the boat, and stating advantages of THAT boat, the salesman should be trying to cure this guy's "Hydrophobia". He should be talking about how they've got a sale on life

vests, and about how the boat is the safest boat on the market, and about how easy it is to learn to swim. THEN talk about buying a boat, and probably won't even need to make a "Special price."

Discover the "Real" reason a person puts up resistance to saying "Yes", and you can deal with it. To do that you must ask a lot of questions, some of them totally unrelated to the product you're trying to sell. Sometimes is doesn't matter what you ask, just **get the person talking to you.** They will eventually tell you all you need to know to hit their "Hot buttons" and stay away from their "Cold zones".

YOUR RESPONSE:

Acknowledge and redirect.

"Ya know, you're a lot like me, it takes me forever to make up my mind to BUY IT (subliminal implant). Now go into at re-pitch of the same earlier pitch, stating all the advantages, etc., and do another close, explaining that tomorrow the xxx will probably not be here, the price will be back up to the non-sale price, that you have a money back guarantee, or any of the other "Drop-closes" you can use. This will give you another opportunity to make another attempted close on the client/customer with probably more positive results.

I HAVE TO WAIT UNTIL...

This is a "Dandy" of one of the most used excuses of evasiveness. They have to "Wait" for one of

20+ reasons, it could be getting paid on a certain date, it could be their wife/husband gets paid on a certain date, or the time of the moon has to be in a certain inclination, and the list is as long as your arm. How do you deal with it?

You always have a response formulated by your home office, your boss, your guru, your company policy etc. That response always starts with the word, "**SURE,**...I understand, the same thing happens to me when I want to make a purchase like this".

YOUR RESPONSE:
"Ya know we can write this up for you so you'll be able to take advantage of this sale, savings, discount etc., and put it over to the side until the date when you want to take delivery, or activate your account" etc. "That way you'll be able to lock this price in for that savings, special price etc."
Now you will find out if that EXCUSE is just useless babble or they are really a buyer. Their instant response will tell you all you need to know about their level of desire in buying. If they hesitate and stammer, it gives you the opportunity to ask them "So you really want the xxx don't you, because it probably won't be here tomorrow?" This tells you who they really are as far as a "Real" buyer.

THE BOX

This is a strategy that has been used to overcome objections since day ONE! You ask them a series of questions BEFORE HAND, which puts them in a box of "Gotta do it or look like a fibber, a liar, a person of lesser credibility. There are 4 questions to ask them like there are 4 sides to a box.

1. Is this something you're interested in?
2. Are you the only decision maker?
3. Do you have the money to do this if you wanted to?
4. Could you take advantage of this sale, price break, in the next 24 hours if you wanted to?

If the answer is YES to all of these questions, then when it comes time for the close - they've got nowhere to go but to say "YES" unless it's just to say, "I've lied to you and I can't do it", and people don't want to do that. They probably just won't answer the phone or not show up for the "Take delivery" meeting. Put them in the "Box" and you will get a higher closure ratio.

JUST DO IT!

OBJECTIONS – OVERVIEW

Objections are only paper tigers to get in the way of closing the sale. Buyers hate to agree with a salesperson, hate to feel like they didn't get that "Special treatment" that their friend got when they bought at the same establishment. So they will say anything to keep from having to say "Yes" to a salesperson. This is in their eyes, just like rolling over and playing dead, quitting without a fight. But fighting what? Is it fighting their self-worth, their self-image and of course their ego? You know as well as anyone the answer to that question is a big YES! They need validation on

their self-worth. But how do they get this validation without taking the other person's head, as in the medieval days?
They get to walk away from the deal with what they THINK is more than they should have gotten, they get something more than someone else got, and they're the "Winner" in that "I paid less and got more" contest!

Some people can never make a decision, one way or the other, and they are so afraid of making the WRONG decision, that making NO decision is the best decision. In an effort to put it off or transfer the decision making responsibility to someone else they go around asking everyone they know about this particular "Thing" or product...until they finally find someone who will tell them not to do it.

Now they don't have to spend that big dollar amount on something they don't really know if they want, need, or can use...THEY THINK!

It's a battle out there. Every time someone wanting to BUY something, interacts with someone trying to SELL something, there is a battle of one degree or another, because they both have a goal that is diametrically opposed to each other's purpose. One person wants to sell something at the highest (or set) price, while the other wants to buy it at the lowest price. What's the solution?

They have to meet somewhere in the middle, while at the same time thinking that each one has

"Put it over" on the other one, or comes away with more that they should have gotten.

It's your job as a closer instead of just an "Order taker" to instill in this customer/client that they ARE coming away with a little "Extra" in their pocket, and not to "Tell anybody" about it". How do you do this? You have your rebuttals to every objection you can think of, as extra "Bullets" in your sales "Gun" or arrows in your sales "Quiver". You select each arrow or bullet based upon the particular objection you come up against, and let it fly. This has got to be as natural as breathing, it has got to APPEAR as if it just came off the top of your head, and you just thought of if it at the moment. It's not something you fabricated, dreamed up or pulled out of the air. Credibility is something that is next to impossible to "Manufacture", mainly because it's so easy to repute and expose as "BS" or fluff.

So, you need to have and then to LEARN these rebuttals to objections absolutely COLD! Practice them in your car, or anywhere there is quiet, and you can "Roll play" with yourself, spitting out these rebuttals like a machine gun. Once again, your job as a salesperson doesn't start until the customer/client says NO, so be ready for an instant fast draw on your "Sales six shooter" to shoot down any of these objections as if they were thieves in the night trying to steal money from your wallet. In truth they are JUST that, and will be doing JUST that if you don't prevent them from becoming REASONS for not buying instead of EXCUSES.

Every time you have an objection you feel you do not address correctly, write it down, and go over it with your supervisor, or determine yourself how to best handle it. Then you have one more bullet in that sales pistol to help you in the battle for those precious words, "Yes I'll take it".

TIP: When receiving objections, allow the other person to talk as much as they want. Eventually they will tell you the deeper meaning or reason they cannot or will not buy at that time.

Almost 90% of the time, the reason/s they're giving you for not buying at the present time are NEVER the actual true reasons for their actions. If you are new to sales, sooner or later when you get beat over the head 10x with this truth, it will finally stick into your brain. You will learn to view it as reality, no matter how real they seem, no matter how sincere they appear to be, you are finally getting the picture. Buyers are liars.

THE BUTTON UP

The ending of the sales experience can make the client feel good about the sale, make them feel that they did the right thing, and will be satisfied with the product or....NOT! Quickly go over the price they were charged, what they got, what to do if they have any questions, give them all phone numbers associated with the home office and what to do if they have any questions. Then THANK THEM FOR THEIR ORDER, and say goodbye!

CHAPTER 5
NEURO-LINGUISTIC PROGRAMMING

Now we are getting in the reason you bought this book in the first place...if you're already in sales. This deals with the REPROGRAMMING of your client/customer and their mental belief system, how they view your product, how they view you in general and what makes them actually say "YES" to the close, when you close.

What if you could actually re-program someone's mind to cause them to see things differently, influence them to view what you say in a more positive aspect, and in general see YOU in a more positive manner rather than just a "Salesperson"?

There are loads of people in the sales profession who do this each day, and have learned the skill of how to walk, talk, and act in a manner that draws client/customers TO them and makes them glad they came, and usually buy what is being sold.

There are other salespeople who accomplish this same result, but they don't know how they do it, or what they are doing when do something right. They only know what they ARE doing works to produce sales and a paycheck.

These people are the ones who over the years have refined what worked down to a science, threw out what didn't work, and they did it because of experience, not because someone came up with a theory of what makes up a subconscious belief system in a customer and tells them to BUY.

Now all of us know about experience, right?

EXPERIENCE AXIOM:
Good judgment comes from experience, and a lot of that comes from bad judgment!

There is a new science of interaction between people discovered by two very forward thinking individuals in the field of psychology. We'll talk about them later, but the overview is, being able to cause your client/customer to view you as someone who cares about them, gives them information in a format and a pace that they like to receive, and in general causes them to view you as someone that they could actually LIKE!

Now you got to admit, anyone with those attributes or views, is a really great sales prospect, and will probably buy whatever you're selling as long as you don't get in the way, and change their mind about the product and YOU.

Before we go too much further you need to soak up some beginning knowledge of NLP and how it affects your daily life, let alone how it can help your efforts at being the top sales person in your business. This is knowledge so powerful that when employed in the field of sales it can double your income without doubling your work efforts.

Yet when I go into a new business that employs a sales staff, and ask them if they know what NLP is, they're answer is usually "Do what now"? It is truly amazing how something that has been around for 25 years or more, can be totally ignored by people who could benefit by it the most. So let's define what it is and how it can make a vast difference in all phases of your life.

WHAT IS NEURO LINGUIST PROGRAMMING?

This is a revolutionary discovery by two individuals John Grinder and Richard Bandler.

NLP was begun in the mid-seventies by a linguist (Grinder) and a mathematician (Bandler) who had strong interests in successful people, psychology, language and computer programming.

It is a difficult to define NLP because those who started it and those involved in it use such vague and ambiguous language that NLP means different things to different people. While it is difficult to find a consistent description of NLP among those who claim to be experts at it, one metaphor keeps recurring. NLP claims to help people change by teaching them to program their brains, and change their belief systems.

So what's a belief system? It is what you truly believe about any subject, not mattering if it is true or not. How you view yourself, your job, your accomplishments, and your potential

An example would be if you are a good putter in golfing and you miss a 3 foot put twice in a row, your personal history has challenged your belief system that you are a good putter...at 3 feet. You can make a 10 foot put just fine, but 3 feet...forget it. Your belief system has changed, and is overriding what you THINK you believe, and have believed in the past.

Once you change your **inward** belief system the outward changes come by themselves automatically if you want them to or not.

In reality, it can change someone's belief system that tells them that they should never by a car with leather seats, to someone who would buy a car, ONLY if it had leather seats. That's reprogramming someone's belief system in the direction YOU want it to go.

We were given brains; but we were given no instruction manual on how to actually use them to the greatest effectiveness.

NLP offers you a users-manual for the brain. The brain-manual seems to be a metaphor for NLP training, which is sometimes referred to as "software for the brain." Furthermore NLP, consciously or unconsciously, relies heavily upon (A) the notion of the unconscious mind as constantly influencing conscious thought and action; (B) metaphorical behavior and speech, especially building upon the methods used in Freud's Interpretation of Dreams; and (C) hypnotherapy as developed by Milton Erickson.

NLP is also heavily influenced by the work of Gregory Bateson and Norm Chomsky.

What does all this mean? It means you can reprogram your potential client/customer to realize the "Advantages" of your product or service in a manner to cause them to **"See"** the advantages, **"Hear"** what you're saying about those advantages, and **"Feel"** more positive toward your product/service, just by the way you talk, act, and react to them.

WHY LEARN NLP TECHNIQUES?

How are all these principals about the way people receive and transmit information useful to salespeople? It can be summed up in one word, called rapport. So let's define rapport.

RAPPORT: When all people involved in a conversation, project, or endeavor, are one with each other in their thinking, efforts, and direction.

In other words, We're all on the "Same page" of enlightenment. Another example is: When your client or potential client truly believes you have his or her best interest at heart, you have what is called rapport. Then people begin to trust you, and when they trust you they BUY from you.

BIAS SYSTEM OF REFERENCE

People use all their senses such as visual, auditory, and kinesthic (feelings) to process information in sending and receiving information.

The point to remember is, different people use ONE of these system more that the other two. The dominant use of this one system of reference out of all three is called their "Bias". The use of this one Bias system predominantly, is what puts them in one of the three categories such as, VISUAL, AUDIO or KINESTIC.

VISUAL A visually biased person likes pictures, sees things when they describe and event, likes words and phrases such as, "Picture this", "Can you see what I'm saying." They are very high energy, animated in their actions, talk with their hands, and their voice goes up when they get excited or want to make a point. Most salespeople are visual and they sell very well to a person who is ALSO visual. As far as closing deals to an audio or kinesthic person, they are not so good.

AUDIO An audio biased person, hears directions and data when they interface with others. They respond well to "I hear what you're saying, this rings my bell, my ears are open." They are less animated, lower energy, talk slower and softer. A high energy visual salesperson had better tone it down here or they're out of luck and it's a no sale.

KINESTHIC This person centers their life around the way they FEEL, and sometimes are very emotional. They respond to phrases like, "I feel very strongly about this", "I feel for you", "I get a good feeling about this." If you think that an AUDIO biased person was slow talking and acting, you'd think this person is dead. You REALLY need to take things slow for this type of person.

However, when you do, you have a friend for life, because they hardly ever meet anyone (let alone a salesperson) that slows down enough to make them comfortable. When and if you do, there is a GREAT chance for a sale.

When a sales person realizes, and can pick up the cues that tell them which bias a person is coming from, it gives them a great advantage on gaining rapport with that person. You begin to use words that fit that person's bias and they have immediate understanding in relation to your presentation. They will have much more understanding of your presentation than they would if you didn't use the "Correct" terminology that aligns with their particular "Bias" VISUAL, AUDITORY or KINISTHETIC.

EXAMPLES:

Visual: Can you SEE your way clear to put down $1000 as a down payment?
Auditory: Just LISTEN to the sound of that xxx, can you HEAR what I'm saying about the $1000 down payment?
Kinesthic: How do you FEEL about $1000 down payment? I can see you've got a good FEELING about this xxx product.

NLP RAPPORT TECHNIQUES

In order to communicate more effectively with anyone on any subject you have to achieve some degree of rapport with them or as they say, "Get on the same page" together. This is the definition of rapport and to get there you need to IDENTIFY the different types of "Bias" that people have formed their lives around. A personality Bias is actually a perceptional view that a person has adopted on which they base their all their value judgments. There are 3 main areas of Bias to take a closer look at when trying to define the term.

3 BIAS TYPES TO IDENTIFY (AS PREVIOUSLY MENTIONED)

VISUAL - Type A type personality - talks faster - voice gets high when excited - uses hands to talk. New Yorkers, Yuppies, high-energy people are visual types. You need to be accelerated in speech, pack a lot into one sentence, use words like "Can you **SEE** your way clear to take advantage of this offer"..."how does this **look** to you". Use words like "See, look, sight, picture that, "See what you're saying" to describe things.

AUDITORY - Slower talker, not as excited or as animated, uses words like hear, sound, rings by bell, "I hear that". Midwesterners, southerners populate this group more than average. You need to slow down, speak softer, use words and phrases like "People like the **sound** of this deal, this might **ring your bell**, can you **hear** what I'm saying in this case". When THEY quit talking, pause for a second and let a silence take up the gap before YOU start speaking. They will begin to relate to you quickly. They may take a little longer to process your information, and ideas you are trying to convey, but it will be worth it to slow down to their level and speed. Since most salespeople are born "Talkers" and run off a the mouth like a machinegun, when this person encounters a salesperson that takes more time, talks slower, and sound "Just like them", when they talk, they LIKE YOU! Take it SLOWER.

KINESTHIC - Very Very Slow, you say "How do you FEEL about that....Doesn't that give you a good feeling....This is how I feel about it." This person is someone who you may never encounter, or come across very infrequently. When you do, if you use this method of speaking, you will gain rapport very quickly, because they always have to deal with people who talk too fast, talk too loud, and never give them a chance to talk. Salespeople being the way they are, (fast talking, high energy, visual types) constantly rub these people the "Wrong way" and find it very difficult to sell this kind of a person. If you tailor your presentation or pitch in this manner to this "Feely, touchy." kind of client you will make a friend instantly. If you think the audio biased person was slow at processing and thinking, you may think this person has died on the phone, or went to sleep. Ask more questions, and go even SLOWER, but try to bring this person up to a little faster level of speaking and interaction. The act of them coming with you (in speed and interaction) is an indication that they are buying YOU, before they buy the product you're selling. SLOW DOWN MORE, to begin with when you talk to one of these.

THE SUBCONSCIOUS MIND

Not enough attention can be given to the subconscious mind, because it has been called the "Seat of all our behavior". This is why we do things for what we later classify as "No good reason". Why we make the wrong choice when we KNOW the right choice, and why we say the wrong things at the wrong time, and later regret them.

The subconscious is a gigantic supercomputer that records each and everything we see, hear, touch, feel, taste and experience. It only records data with no inflections on speech, or colorations. It's like you are writing on a blackboard and someone else reads it with no expression or puts anything in context. So if you say things in response to a client's statement when THEY say "I don't want to buy it for $125 today", and you say, (trying to drop-close them)"Not even for $49?", the subconscious mind only realizes the phrase, *"NOT EVEN FOR $49"*, which turns that phrase into a command...a command that says, **they do not want it...** "Not even for $49." Never use contractions, they are negative words, and should be ELEMINATED from all your speech and pitch.

If it has an apostrophe, it is a contraction and it carries a negative value. Examples are: CAN'T, WON'T, DON'T, SHOULDN'T, COULDN'T SHANT, WOULDN'T, HAVEN'T, ISN'T and all of these should be eliminated in any part of your pitch, rebuttals, or presentation.

When you eliminate all the contractions from your speech or pitch you cannot repeat back to that person the reason they just gave you for not buying.

EXAMPLE: They say "I can't buy it now I don't have the money." Now if you're really a newbie, and really stupid, you repeat back, *"Oh you can't buy it now because don't have the money?"* If you never said can't or don't you would not repeat what they just told as a reason why they could not buy.

IMPORTANT INFORMATION

Analog Marking Embedded Commands

How the subconscious takes in information.

Picture all your speech as sound bites on a screen. It may look like a picket fence, with all the little vertical pickets, in a row. The words that are said in a louder, softer, or different volume, or said with an accompanying sound (like a tap on a table) create a "Spike" above all the rest. This "Spike" sticks up higher, and is seen by the subconscious more readily. So if you increase or decrease your volume on certain words you "Mark" them to stand out in the subconscious mind. When I was selling subscriptions to an investment newspaper, I said things like… "If you make money with the paper you'll **buy the paper** (said at a faster pace) and we want to get you to **make money** (slightly louder) as fast as possible. **You...(pause) like me** (at a slower pace), understand that to make good decisions you need good information, and **by now** (louder volume) you realize the importance of this. You have just embedded the commands**:**

- **BUY THE PAPER**
- **MAKE MONEY**
- **YOU LIKE ME**
- **BUY NOW**

All of a sudden your client/customer is thinking, *"I dunno what it is about this guy, but I'm start'in to like him".* The next thing he says is "So what do I gotta do, give you a credit card or someth'n". DONE DEAL...imbedded commands! **USE THEM!**
This stuff is scary, and it works! The trick is, how you can incorporate the phrases you specifically need into your own pitch, practice them until they become second nature, and throw them in at just the right time.

Suddenly your closure ratio will drastically improve, and this new ability will translate itself into more new accounts, more sales and greater customer satisfaction.

The trouble is, it takes a lot of WORK. You need to think of the things you want to accomplish with your script, identifying the buyer profile, identifying interest, the necessary funds to spend, and controlling the sales situation.
Write them out in short phrases and try including them in between phrases that you normally use.

Some suggestions are:

- BUY NOW
- BUY IT
- BUY TONIGHT/TODAY
- YOU LIKE ME
- FEEL GOOD
- ORDER NOW
- LIKE IT
- GREAT FEELING
- IT'S SAFE

Here is an example of incorporating embedded commands in a presentation. The commands are in bold text.

When you **WRITE A CHECK** for a new product, service, car/copier/refrigerator etc. it's a big purchase and you need to **FEEL GOOD** about it, and **BUY NOW** I think you've researched the product well enough to know xxxx etc. **BUY NOW** you've probably realized that... I think **YOU**...(pause) **LIKE ME**...agree that this product is right up there in the ratings and this is one of the things that make people want to **BUY IT. BUY TODAY**, or **BUY** the end of the day/night this xxx will be gone, and we have no more in stock...etc. "I think **IT'S SAFE**...to believe this xxx will do the job for you. People **LOVE** ... the fact that you can do xxxx with this product, and when you **GET IT**, you will too.

You need to deliver these phrases with the proper phrasing, pausing, and volume on each word each of the command words (in bold). When the subconscious "Sees" these embedded phrases and commands it will, before very long, filter these messages up to the conscious mind and the "I'll take it" response comes out of their mouth.

IMPORTANT INFORMATION

MIRRORING

This is you in your physical body making a mirror image of the person in front of you. If you look like, act like, talk like, and are a mirror of that person, you WILL achieve a very high level of rapport with them almost instantly. If they stand with more weight on one leg, with one hand in their left pocket, so do you. If they are sitting behind their desk with their elbows on the each arm of the chair and their fingers "Steepled" together, so do you. It sets up a "He/she's just like me", syndrome, and who wouldn't want to buy from someone just like themselves?

Someone just like them would NEVER lie, inflate product claims, or stretch the truth, right? When done correctly this should be declared illegal, and may well be someday...but not today!

MATCHING

This is nothing more than copying someone's manner. Walking like they walk, talking the way they talk with the same speed and cadence. Be careful though when you go trying to match their accent, you'd better be REALLY good at it because if not you will be exposed as a phony, and everyone hates a phony. This will be the end of your chance to sell this person.

PACING

This is adopting the other person's speed of reactions. If they talk slower, so do you, if they react slower, you slow down. Then when you've locked on to their pace, you speed up (in all areas) a little bit and see if they follow you. If they do, you know you have affected their behavior, and they are going along with you. Now just lead them into the close, and finish the sale. They will come out feeling like they did the right thing, bought the right product/service, and be one "Happy camper".

These things are the basis of gaining rapport, and intern someone's confidence. When you do this, if they fit the profile of a buyer (interest, money, desire) you have got a 90% chance of closing the deal.

Just remember to USE this every chance you get. This is the hard part in learning to alter your sales style, behavior, and closing techniques. Once again, LEARNING is the APPLICATION of knowledge acquired.

JUST DO IT!

CHAPTER 6
TYPES OF BUYERS

Almost every "How to" sales book has a chapter or section on how to sell to different types of buyers, what they look for, how they process of information, and what motivates them. That's great, but there is one chapter they always leave out, because up until a few years ago "They" didn't even know this process existed. This is a process derived from a relatively new discovery previously mentioned in the above chapter called Neuro-Linguist Programming.

It's called a person's BIAS. A bias is how a person arranges the WAY they process information, or how they LIKE to receive information. The three main types of biases: **Visual, Auditory, Kinesthetic.**

We will talk more about them in a second. Some ways people receive information makes them feel comfortable and other ways make them feel UNcomfortable. Which way would YOU like to receive information, comfortably or uncomfortably? Which way would make you want to buy from someone, being comfortable or uncomfortable with them? Have you ever been with a salesperson that made you feel uncomfortable? Did you buy from them? Of course not, and you probably sought out a salesperson that made you feel comfortable, at home, and at ease, right?

If the truth be said, that salesperson was

probably not "Working" at making you feel comfortable, they were just that type of person that people could feel comfortable around, enjoyed being around, and never seemed to work at causing people to like them.

Why are they this way, and how do they do what they do so well as far as making you feel comfortable, is the whole subject of gaining rapport and what NLP is all about. WHY are these master closers the 5% who sell the 90% of the business?

First let's take the issue of how they accomplish making you feel comfortable just being around them.

What is comfort anyway? It's being at ease, not feeling pressure, knowing there is an open door you can walk out at any time. On top of all that, you have a rapport with the person you're talking to or in this situation, the salesperson you are working with. So let's define rapport. Rapport is when the other person involved in the conversation, situation, or interaction makes you feel like they actually CARE about your satisfaction, your views, and your well being. Now you feel at ease, and once again...comfortable, but how do they achieve rapport with you to begin with? It may be the first time you meet them, they don't know your likes, dislikes, personality, or anything about you that would make you like them, but still you do.

This person has mastered, Mirroring, Matching,

Pacing, Imbedded commands (that have been mentioned earlier) and more. The funny thing is, most of the top sellers don't know actually how they do it, they just do it. If they actually thought about HOW they did it, they would probably have the same problem as the proverbial centipede that when he tried to figure out how he moved all of this 24 legs in perfect timing to get him across the ground...suddenly couldn't walk.

In other words, it just comes naturally to these top sellers, and now this "Natural ability" has been broken down into it's component parts, defined specifically, and synthesized so that it can be taught to anyone willing to spend some time learning, and they call it, NLP.

In this publication, however, we ARE going to break it down for you and show you how to synthesize the actions of the top sellers and be able to duplicate their actions time after time to put you up on top with them and most likely break their sales records, and closure percentages. This is because it's not rocket science; it's not that difficult to do what they do, once you see it clearly for what it is.

So...let's break it down and dissect what they do starting with the types of people we sell to and their characteristics.

As we mentioned earlier there are three types of biases, visual, auditory, and Kinesthetic, so let's explore each of these types and lean how they "Like" to receive information and how they process this information they receive to decide if they want to buy or "Think about it".

VISUAL PERSON

This person is the typical A type personality, they are high strung, fast paced, fast talking, "Give me the bottom line" type of person. This is the way they like to get their incoming data, quick, concise, and no candy coating or "BS."

They use pictures to relate to what is being said to them. Draw them a picture and they are with you all the way. Their voice goes up and octave when the get excited, and use their hands a lot when they talk, even on the phone. Which is the mark of a total amateur in phone sales because no one can see your hands when you're talking on the phone, and it's a waste of energy. Yet some people do it. This person responds to VISUAL words like "See, look, eyes, clear", and other visual related words. If you use these words in describing your product this person will "See what you're saying" and your chances of getting a sale are greatly increased.

AUDITORY PERSON

This person is more laid back, and they arrange their world around what they HEAR. They talk slower, very little animation in their gestures, and their voice remains on an even keel most of the time. They use and respond to words like, hear, sound like, ring your bell, and other audio related terms. Use phrases like, "How does this sound to you, or this has a good ring to it", etc., and you increase you chances of a "Yes" at the close.

Your speed of word per minute is very important with this person. They like things slow, so S L O W D O W N. If you are a high energy fast talker, unless you change your pitch to accommodate this audio biased person you WILL strike out and wonder why.

You need to listen very carefully to the words this person uses, because they will most likely give you a clear sign that they are AUDIO biased by using audio related words in their speech. Examples would be:

- I like the SOUND of that
- That's music to may ears
- That rings my bell
- I hear what you're saying
- That's an earful
- You sound like you know xxxx

When you come in contact with this type of person and you begin to use the correct bias generated phrases, you will make a friend quickly, because most people never talk slow enough, walk slow enough and react slow enough for this person to feel comfortable around.

When they finish a sentence, let a short time of silence exist before you reply, it will make a major difference in your relationship with this person, be it professional or personal.

They also dislike irritating sounds in their immediate environment, like loud stereos with thumping music, or wrap. So if you know you've got one of these types or discover their AUDIO bias soon into your relationship, turn the background noise or radio or whatever down, it will make a big difference to this person and probably be worth a sale to you.

KINESTHETIC PERSON

This person resembles someone who would be classified as the "Walking dead." If you thought audio biased people were slow, or low key, kinesthetic biased people make audio biased people look like a rocket on the end of a stick!

Very few people are kinesthetic in their bias toward life and surroundings, but when you get one and you match and mirror them, it most likely will be one of the few times they will be mimicked in their mannerisms and will respond very positively if they are inclined at all to buy what you're selling.

This person is extremely laid back, low key and very slow in their speech, and mannerisms. They arrange most of their life, and decisions around the way they FEEL. If it feels right do it...is their slogan. So to make it "Feel right" you need to use words like...FEEL, touch, good feeling about this, hold on to it, etc. The most important thing is to remember to ...slow down.... and talk slower, checking all the time to see if they heard you, are "With" you, and are following along.

This is the hardest person to sell, because they never get someone who is willing to match them in speed of speech, and mannerisms, and usually "Hate salesmen" because of it. So when you do match their slowness and talk in the words that make them FEEL comfortable, you've got a great chance for a "Yes" at the close.

POSITIVE / NEGITIVE PERCEPTIONS

Here is one very important division on people that governs the way the make decisions about buying, and about life.

In this instance we are not talking about their attitude being positive or negative, we are talking about their view of all events as it relates to them and their situation. Meaning in this case they are drawn TO, or motivated by the POSITIVE thing or event they will gain by doing something or making a certain choice. They go TOWARD something because it is positive in their perception.

POSITIVE TYPE PERSON

For this person you would point out all the *benefits* of a product or service and how they would enjoy having or using it, more than showing them how it would SAVE them from something that they DIDN'T want to have happen.

They don't consider the negative aspect of something or an event as much as the see the positive side of it. They buy a car because of the way it exhilarates them when they get behind the wheel, not because it's safe and protective, even if it is the safest car on the road. They like going TOWARD the positive more than they like running AWAY from the negative.

NEGITIVE TYPE PERSON

The negative person is easy to spot, they are the whiner, they are the, "I don't know if I should" type, they use words like can't, won't, shouldn't, couldn't, and all the negative contractions. They need to get TOLD what they want, and they WANT to be told what they need!

Some times they will actually ask you, "Do you think I should buy this"? This is the person you focus on telling how the product or service will PROTECT them or their interests, keep from loss, give them a shelter, and insure or secure their position.

Their whole life is about running AWAY from the negative, being afraid of losing what they have, and they have a great FEAR factor governing their life. It's up to you to remove that fear and replace it with strength and protection. Never *ask* this person if they WANT to buy what you're selling, just **tell** them, "Buy the 3 year subscription" or "Buy the red one, you'll love it!" When you do tell them the best choice for them, do it in a command voice or manner, using very few words. Not "Well, I think you should probably buy the xxxx", but **"BUY THE xxx ONE! YOU'LL BE GLAD *YOU'RE GETTING IT*"** (embedded command in italics)

It is more important for them to buy something that keeps them from harm, rather that something that will bring them enjoyment. It is VERY IMPORTANT that you recognize and separate these two types of personalities.
When you know if a person a "Positive valence"

type person, you talk about how a product will benefit them, help them, and get them ahead.

On the other hand, when you realize you have a "Negative valence" person in front of you, you stress how a product or service will PREVENT them from loss, harm, and PROTECT them from losing what they have. Or you stress what a great warranty the product has, or freedom from breakage or down time. This will get you much farther toward a sale with this type of person, but you need to recognize which is which.

It's easy to see which one is + and which one is – just by noticing their speech, level of confidence, and how they view their life and situations. The positive person is definitive, concise, doesn't use a lot of filler words and sounds (er, aha, ohm, I ah, well aha, ya but etc), they seem to know what they want and all you have to do is guide them to what they already want to do, while pointing out the POSITIVE aspects of the product or service. They quickly will evaluate the product, what you have said, and if they have the money, they end up closing themselves.

Once again there is a very important element involved here, that we have talked about earlier, and will talk about a lot...LISTENING. If you have done your job of slowing down, taking in the information they have imparted to you, evaluated it and assigned value to parts of it, you will know how to sell each one. So...JUST DO IT!

SELLING AS RELATED TO PARTICULAR PROFESSIONS OR JOBS

So now that you know the types of biases that people organize their life and their buying habits around, let's explore the different types of people and what motivates them to buy or not buy. The easiest was to separate buyer types is to separate them as to their professions, which sometimes go hand in hand with the types of bias that they use to: look, listen, or feel...the world.

If you made divisions of people types you come up with just a few major categories, and the main ones are:
Technical types and non-technical types, care givers, and helpers, entrepreneurs and leaders. Each one of these categories possesses certain characteristics that motivate that person to buy or hold back.

THE ENIGNEER

This person is a calculator of information and or events. They are methodical and need hard cold facts to support the claims of a product or service. If you give them these hard cold facts it doesn't matter if they don't have the money, were shy in purchasing, or have any other hurdles to buying, they will turn around and say, "Yes". How can you ague with the "Truth?" The product is 27.5% better at what it does compared to it's competition, is 16% better at reliability, and has been chosen by 22% more of the people (Just like him) who looked at it, and therefore how can he or she refuse it.

This person is very hard to BS, if you try to come at them with anything but facts you ...will...loose.

Knowing this, don't try to fabricate information about the product, they probably know more than you do about it. Just try to find out if they know ALL the facts, and are there things that they DON'T know about the product or service? The instant you enlighten them with new information they were not aware of, you double the chance for a sale.

Just give them the facts and maybe a personal story about a customer that previously bought the xxx and loved it, if you have one. It's also good to ask them where they went to school, and if you have a common ground there in geographic, or similar academic background that's a great ice breaker or great help in gaining rapport.

THE EDUCATOR

This person is a teacher, and also a student, and they need to know WHY. Why is your product better, they are the ultimate question asker. They also find it very hard to make up their mind, and this is where you come in. Make it up FOR them. Answer their questions, and then simply take out your pen or ask how many they would like to order. The assumed close works very well with them once they've been shown all the options.

When you find out they are a teacher or professor etc., ask what they taught, and try to come up with scenario that relates to your educational experience, one of your teachers, or mentors, and how they helped you in some way. This goes a long way to achieve rapport with this type of individual, and once again...people buy from someone they like, and they WILL like you.

THE DOCTOR

He or she is a "Helper" type of person. People don't become doctors **just** because they want to make a lot of money, there first has to be a level of giving, a level of helping and they have a "It's not always about ME", attitude.

The Doctor likes to be CALLED "Doctor" first of all, especially the *pseudo* doctors like chiropractors or podiatrists. I say pseudo doctors because they are looked down upon by actual medical doctors who have done years of internship and have residency at a hospital or started an actual practice as a "Medical Doctor". These "Near" doctors like to be called doctor, more than all the rest and they will tell you. So...when you are trying to sell one these you really *want to* call them "DOCTOR", all the time. This will get you a long way. Doctors are not really technically minded although they are very detailed minded. They have to be this way in their profession because of the complex issues they face every day. So if your are trying to sell a doctor a piece of software that will make it easier to him to do billing, you had better be working with his office manager, or the person responsible for that particular aspect of his practice. In fact, the chances that you will actually be able to talk to the doctor...are too slim to even calculate! So concentrate on the office manager and when you win her over, you're at second base.

THE NURSE

This person (male or female), like the doctor, is a caregiver, open and honest in their dealings and places a high degree of importance on credibility, and honesty. They are in the business of helping people and although they might not be super adept at dealing with sales tactics and closing techniques, they can spot a "Phony" a mile away.

They don't have the academic background of the doctor, and although you do not need to have a 4 year degree to attain your RN status, most registered nurses do have a BS to be able to compete for jobs in the market place. A lot of nurses fit in the "Feeling" category of personalities, which means they make buying decisions on how they FEEL about a product/service. A lot of technical data, and specifications are not important to them. They are the typification of the emotional buyer, and make their decision to buy on how the product/service grabs them EMOTIONALLY.

They would probably buy a stereo speaker because of the way it LOOKS, and how it would relate to their room décor, rather than how it SOUNDS.

In presenting your product to this type person you need to dwell on the level of COMFORT the product is going to give them, and the level of security and piece of mind it will give them. They are helpers to others first, and themselves second.

They would like to receive the same treatment from you that they give to their patients/clients. YOU have to be a helper with the attitude that your commission or the sale is on the "Back burner" of importance to you, and use a very careful "Lack of pressure" closing technique for this person.

They don't "Color outside the lines" and are not super creative, thinking in advance of the many different ways the product will benefit them. They tend to be a "Follow the rules" type of person so don't overload them with detailed technical data about the product, this will only confuse them and end they end they will "Have to think about it."

Just point out the main advantages, paint the picture of them already having, using, and enjoying the product/service, then give them the pen to "Sign here", and wait for their response.

THE LAWYER

This person is a master with words, thinks two steps ahead of you, and is always thinking how you are trying to screw him over, because he makes his living screwing OTHER people over, or finding the crack in their defenses, and exposing their weaknesses. This person has to be handled with care, NEVER lied to, and don't even stretch the truth with him/her, they'll find out and you're dead meat.

If you and present a clear picture of the benefits, how it helps AND keeps this person from harm, being taken advantage of, or jeopardized in any way, you will go along way with them. They are both positive and negatively pollarded so going toward the positive and away from the negative will put you in a good position to sell this client.

When interacting with attorneys it is best to let them have "The floor" all the time when they start talking. They talk for a living, just like you do, but people shut up when they start to speak, because they have the floor during a court proceeding, and feel like they have the floor whenever they open their mouth.

They usually will ask you questions, and these are questions you were getting ready to answer in the form of statements before they became questions. Now you get to REact to this person with the answers to questions you already knew BEFORE the questions were asked. So, it's like being in a contest when you know what your opponent's next move will be BEFORE they make it. When they do, you are all prepared for the response, and PRETEND it just came off the top of your head, which makes you look like you are very well versed on the product, and your field in general. This intern says, "Credibility", and lawyers like credibility.

You can respond with statements like, "You know, I'm glad you asked that question" or, "That's a great question"...

Just let him/her ramble on in their oratorical manner (they love the sound of their own voice) and supply the needed information when asked. Pretty soon they will begin to think, "I like this salesperson, they don't keep rambling on because they just like the sound of their own voice!"

This personality type will actually sell themselves, because they base their buying decisions on FACTS. They put all the facts together, weigh them, add them up, divide by the quantity, get an average, and if that average says, "Good deal", they are reaching for their wallet.

Pretty soon when they are done, all you will need to say is "Will that be Visa or MasterCard".

TRUCK DRIVER BLUE COLLAR WORKER

A very hard worker, prides himself/herself on honesty, integrity, and truth. The salt of the Earth, and is very short on trust, because he's been "Taken" so many times by the "System" as he calls it. Possibly drinks a little too much, takes relaxing to a new level when away from work. He places a very high value on family, kids, and "Providing" for his wife and children. Doesn't have a lot of spending money so is very reluctant to part with any of it and will have to be "Bonded with" in order to make a sale. So mirroring, matching and pacing are in order for this potential client. If you walk like, talk like and be...like this guy or girl...your chances are good, but they can tell a "Fake" a mile away, so unless you got your "Country boy" accent down really good just keep it simple for this one and you'll go a long way.

THE SALESMAN

Now this one could be the easiest or toughest sale you're ever going to make. It depends on how you work it. A salesman / woman, likes to be sold, and they know how to play the game of salesman, and client.
They probably know every trick in the book (like this one) because they've read every "Book" there is on selling and you're not going to pull any "Wool over their eyes" as they put it, so don't try. They know all the "Urgency" tricks to get them to buy now, the "If I could would you" techniques and phrases, so the best thing to do is just give it to them straight. The old..."This is the deal, and this is what it costs, and here's what'chagotta pay at the end, and that's what I can do for you" type of attitude.

They'll appreciate the honesty and pretty soon you have a new client, and they respect your up front attitude. The reason is, you didn't try to use the same tricks on them that they use every day on everybody else. The questions they are going to ask you will be more about the price terms, conditions, and options for payment. Most likely they have researched the product or service, and now as much about it as you do. If they don't they will want to pick your brains for every last bit of information they can, before making a decision to buy, but the most determining factor for this person will probably be the price. Since they make their living by selling something, they know the "Drill". Buy for as LITTLE as possible, sell it for as MUCH as possible. That is the code that they live by, and that's the bottom line for them at the end of the day.

THE BUSINESS OWNER

In you are in the B to B field (business to business) and your primary focus is selling to other businesses, you are in for a "Herculean" task. So here are a few of the major walls, pitfalls, and whoops you will have to jump through and hurdles you need to deal with.

TIME: A business owner is usually providing a service to someone or group, and their livelihood is making THESE people happy and satisfied, not talking to YOU! The only way you can get their attention is to impress upon them in the first 30 seconds, how whatever you're selling will help them...help THEIR customer/clients, better, faster, more efficiently, and improve their profit margin.
You need to realize that most of the time you call them, that you are about the 3rd of 4th call trying to sell them the same service or product, so you better have a unique pitch, or slant on YOUR product or service in a way that blows away anything else that's out there.
Most of the time when (if you actually GET to talk to the owner) they grant you and audience they are also dealing with a customer either in person or on the other line. You...a salesperson...are the last person they want to talk to, because you're taking them away from someone who may, or WILL result in money coming into their company, or worst, may take money FROM their company unless they get satisfied. The person who has a problem with the owner is obviously griping to him, agitating him/her, and putting them in a less

that happy mood, and now in answering the other line they get you, a SALESPERSON! Is it any wonder you'd better have a good opening line?

So how do you structure your opening statement? You make it short and to the point. You don't ask them how their day is going, or how are they doing? They don't care that YOU are pretending to care how their day is going, or how they are doing. They realize, now they've got a salesman on the phone that is trying to gain rapport with them so they can sell them something they may not need, or want.

THE "I NEED YOU INTRO"

If you are selling a piece of equipment or service that they already use and it would be better, more efficient, cost less than what they now use, you can start by asking them if they perform THIS service or have this certain capability. Now they think that **you** may want to hire them to do this, and they (or their gate keeper) have a much more positive initial perception of you. Bottom line, you've got their attention, and their TIME.

EXAMPLE: I was selling a lease program for copy machines to print shops and copy shops. Some business with the name "Printing" in the title only do large quantity printing and don't ever want or need a copy machine. That was the first level of qualification, so without just coming out and asking, "Do you need a copy machine", (because they would always say "NO", even if they did) I started my pitch by asking if they made short run copy jobs on a copy machine. Instantly they thought I wanted to hire them to do some printing, so the ones who DID make short run digital jobs would of course say, "Yes, how can I help you"? Then I proceeded to tell them how our lease program on REFERBISHED but almost new copy machines could save them hundreds of dollars a month with all the maintenance included, and the next thing I know, they are asking me what kind of machines we have to lease.

When dealing with businesses you must realize that the most important thing to them is TIME, and the second most important thing to them, are their customers/clients. As long as you can either give them more time by creating more efficiency in doing what they now do, or bring them more clients that represent more money, they WILL TALK TO YOU!

CHAPTER 7
USING THE TELEPHONE

The term "Telephone sales" conjures up all type of images for most people, most of them negative, and why not. There are more scams being sold by phone that any other mode of selling. Certain states (Florida especially) have very loose laws and constraints governing the use of a telephone as a sales tool. The FCC (Federal Communications Commission) now has strict laws (rarely enforced) about what you can and cannot do in calling potential customers/clients on the phone.

People can file a complaint by phone or on line to the FCC once they get the name and phone number of the company, then an investigative file is created and the company is under some degree of scrutiny. There now is a measure of phone abuse prevention, called the "Don't call list", on which you can list your name and phone number and then are not "Suppose" to get telemarketing calls. Once again it doesn't seem to do any good at preventing unwanted calls from the "Telephone salesman" or company that has a "Predictive dialer." This predictive dialer is dialing 200 phone numbers a minute from a list that you happen to get on when you put your name and phone number on that drawing to win a prize, or register your newly purchased product or device. There are strict rules that a company must adhere to when using one of these dialers or face retribution and possible fines from the FCC.

However; because it is significantly difficult to

actually apprehend the culprits in the act of violating the rules, and or calling the "Don't call" names, we're back to much of the same status quo as no rules at all. The bottom line is, how to use the phone to MAKE MONEY *without* violating these rules, and making a lot of people mad at you!

If you are new to the phone as a sales tool, then this book was written for you. This chapter is the most important one that will increase your closure rate, make you the King/Queen of your "Room", or sales team etc. It will give you more options to use to deal with the objections of your potential client/customer on the telephone, and just in general more options at presenting the opportunity and ways to close that difficult sales prospect.

TELEMARKETING

First of all if you think you are going to elevate your vocational job status in life by calling it "Phone sales" or "Inside sales executive", understand one thing...it's telemarketing, you're a telemarketer, you call people on the phone who you don't know and try to get money from them in some way.

It always is, and always has been an industry plagued by dishonesty, inflated claims, and bothersome salespeople who have discovered that it does pay considerable returns if you're good at what you do.

It's just like almost any field you can mention, in sales there are good salespeople and there are bad salespeople. The worst thing is that the very few bad salespeople give the entire sales force a general reputation that is impossible to change once someone experiences that level of negative interaction.

LABELS

Why does the label "Used car salesman" conjure up a preconceived picture of a short, fat, bald guy wearing a polyester plaid suit with a loud tie that doesn't match anything he's wearing including his underwear? Because that's what 3% of the used car salesmen look like, (in Florida) and that's all people remember when they think about, talk about, and relate to ANY car salesman.

But let's face the facts, it doesn't matter to most of us what kind of a label we wear when we're brining down 6 figures a year, driving a new "Vet", and the person with a law degree from Harvard can't find a job right out of school.

So, guess what *they* do? They get a telemarketing job, and learn from the boss how to talk to people, (something they didn't learn at Harvard) and start making 6 figures a year. THEN they become the attorney for the telemarketing firm, for a bigger 6 figure income.

However, let's get down to the real world where

we all live and talk about "Raking it in", because that's why you're reading this book to begin with.

That's it, it's nothing different, and there are people who make a lot of money at it. But...it's one of the toughest jobs out there, and you have to have as tough a "Skin" to keep at it, pounding the phone, smiling and dialing.

VERY few people make that high paycheck every week, even though the ads for "Inside salesmen" boast about how you can make $10,000 a month or more at this "Easy sale" account rep position.
So let's take a very close look at "Telemarketing" and break it down into a few parts that may be a little bit easier to understand. Everybody who is out of work, whatever their "Regular" work is, thinks all you have to do to make money at telephone sales is call people up, (usually at dinner time because they're home then), read a pre-written script into the phone and get paid.
If it were that simple, everybody would be in telephone sales making tons of money!

Those people out of their "Regular" job see an ad that says, *"Dream job, make $5000 a month, easy sale"*, and they can't wait to be one of the 200 people that respond, because they haven't thought, "If it were that simple, everybody would be in telephone sales making a ton of money!

When they find that they have to make about 100 calls to get one person who won't hang up on them, suddenly they begin to realize something. This is TOUGH, and the only people that actually

MAKE money at it have refined their skill and have a little thing called work ethic! Which means, they show up every day, on time, get on the phone and dial the numbers of leads they are assigned, and just talk to a LOT of people.

After that, they begin to apply the principals of selling, most of which are within these pages, and they get their first deal. Now they're hooked.

2 SIDES OF THE "COIN" THE SAME

When you look at the concept of PHONE SALES, and break it down to its main parts, we would want to look at both sides of the telephone "Coin", called advantages and disadvantages.

ADVANTAGES

No one can see you. In the "Face to face" world of selling, people make predeterminations about you instantly on the first meeting because of how you LOOK. What is your dress, body type, haircut/style, weight and facial expressions. If you're not the snappy dresser, have an "In shape" body, great smile, and warm handshake, nobody knows.

It's your VOICE that carries you to closing a deal. That's why this book spends so much time and text on the characteristics of your voice. You can be anyone you want to be on the phone, with just a little work and practice. You could be in your pajamas or bathrobe (and some people are) making sales right and left. If you're good at "Mirroring" (talked about previously) you can sound just like the person you're talking to on the other end of the line. Now who wouldn't want to buy from someone just like themselves?

On the phone you can paint a better picture with less distractions. When you are telling someone about your product or service, it's all AUDIO. They begin to SEE your descriptions more vividly because there are no other pictures, or distractions in their sphere of influence. They could be looking into a wall, or a desk, or any immediate environment that is static, non-moving and most important non-distracting. So, use this aspect of the telephone selling experience to your advantage, and paint the picture, describe the scene as if you are trying to describe the sunset to a blind person who never has seen a sunset. If you can do this you are on your way to being known as a Master Closer.

DISADVANTAGES

No one can see you

Now you are probably saying to yourself, "Didn't I just read that?" If you have that winning smile, the "Together" look, and a warm handshake...FORGET IT. It won't make any difference, all of your warmth, personality, and countenance won't make a bit of difference if you can't make it come across in your VOICE.

So where to you put your energy and emphasis? Again, you put it in your VOICE. I've been in phone rooms (some of the time around amateur salespeople) and you see them waving their hands around, making gestures trying to describe a device, or pounding on their desk (which by the way is bad because it's irritating to everyone else), and I guess they think that this is going to help them get a sale. NOT! **PEOPLE CAN'T SEE YOU!**

So I try to help them by saying, "Put your energy in your VOICE not your hands". Five minutes later, they're still waving their hands around. It's like talking to a cat! Sit on your hands if you have to (providing you're using a headset) and try to describe or sell without the use of any gestures, it WILL make you better at USING your voice as an effective instrument of persuasion, instead of just talking.

TWO SIDED INTERACTION

People who receive "Your type" of phone call get these calls every day, and usually the gate keeper/secretary is suppose to filter these calls. If she puts you through to the decision maker (which says a lot about you) you have one chance. Make YOUR call different from all the other calls this person responds to, and usually hangs up on, or dismisses.

You agree that it's a sales call and that you know they get a deluge of these types of calls and you are very appreciative of the fact that they TOOK your call in the first place. This will go a long way to put them at some degree of ease and probably give you another 10 seconds of time before they blow you off. Because...you acknowledge this and sound like a "No pressure" type of person they may give you another 10 seconds of their time to develop a "POTENTIAL client relationship". SLOW...DOWN! If you relax, THEY might relax. Remember, you can't say the wrong thing to the right person, and if they ARE the right person, they have a remote interest in what you're selling, and you sound DIFFERENT from all the other "Idiots" that call him/her, you may do some good with this call. You state the advantages of your product, why they need you or your company, how much they will save by doing business with you. Then ask well thought out question that will get them to stay on the line, when they were just going to hang up.

Make it TWO...SIDED conversation. If you can get them talking, you have scaled the first wall of resistance, maybe found their level of interest, and that's the first main hurdle.

INCOMING AND OUTGOING CALLS

If you were to rate all sales jobs on their degree of difficulty, telephone sales would have to rank as the most difficult. Let's examine why.

FACE TO FACE ADVANTAGES

In FTF (Face To Face) you can obviously see the person and you can use your charming facial expressions like smiling* to gain rapport with a client or potential customer. In phone sales or telemarketing it's an entirely different set of challenges. Nobody can see your face, nobody knows if you're short, fat, bald, have a polyester suit on, or in a lot of cases, in your bathrobe

NO FACE TO FACE

Now let's consider the OTHER side of the coin, which means you CANNOT see the other person's face, body language, and mannerisms. This is a big disadvantage for you, because these elements are how you can judge if they are interested, telling the truth, and in general where their buying signals start and stop. Without seeing their face and body language, you have less of a frame of reference, and the only thing you have to go on is their VOICE.

The only thing you have to gain rapport with, and make the sale, is YOUR VOICE. So let us examine how to USE this audio projection of your personality to get the job done. There are several critical areas to consider in the phone sales business.

VOLUME

The volume of your voice is one of the most important areas of phone sales. If it's too soft and people can't hear you, they cannot understand your pitch, and have no idea of what you are talking about.

Since just about every person you talk to DOES NOT want to talk to a salesman, especially on the phone, and even more so if it's an unsolicited call, you'd better have a perfect volume to your voice.

Make sure it's not too loud or soft, and you can even ask someone, "Can you hear me ok"? Then 99% of the time they will give you their first "Yes", which is a good habit to get them into.

POSITIVE ANSWER SYNDROME:
When you ask a question of a prospective client/customer you had better formulate it so that the answer is always YES!

This gets the client/customer into the habit of SAYING yes. From then on, you keep asking questions that most likely will generate a yes. This continues to get them in the framework of saying yes, which for a salesperson is A...GOOD...THING!

Some salespeople are actually too loud, and I can't understand why they think they have to scream into the phone unless their client/customer actually has a hearing problem. I guess it makes them feel like they are projecting more of a "Forceful" personality, and this is suppose to get them more deals? THEY need this book more that anyone else, but will probably never seek out sales training because they "Know everything they need to know." So they drive everyone else in the room crazy because the other salespeople can't hear the person they are talking to on THEIR phone call. If you are on the phone in a room of other salespeople take that into consideration, then hopefully you won't get fired on your first day.

You can regulate your volume to accent certain areas of your pitch. For instance, if you want to attach great importance to a phrase or line, LOWER the volume considerably at that time. It makes it sound like you are telling the client/customer a secret that nobody but them should hear, and they are privileged to be hearing it.

It also tells you if they are listening if they ask you to repeat it because they didn't hear all of it. Vary the volume of your voice when delivering your pitch, otherwise it sounds like a recorded robot, and people wonder if you're READING your pitch, which is the WORST thing to have happen. Now they perceive you as a boiler room, telemarketing slave, who knows only what you are reading, are only interested in a commission and probably will say anything to get a sale. Stop and pause with a "And ah, this is a ah"....to make it SOUND like you're doing this off the top of your head. SOUNDING real is much more important than anything else in the credibility aspect of telephone sales. Sound real and you will close deals.

TONEALITY

The tone of your voice is another very important part of gaining rapport with someone on the phone. A good way of determining the tonality you use, is to record several of your sales calls. Normally it is illegal to record a call with someone unless you tell the person in advance, but since you're just recording for your own information to listen to yourself, that's not necessary. Some people have a voice that resembles a buzz saw going through knotty pine hitting a rusty nail, or something like that. If you have less than a smooth, pleasing voice dripping with honey, then you need to practice with tonality.

What makes good tonality? Ask yourself the question, "Which is more pleasing, a high pitched monotone voice sounding like fingernails on a blackboard, or a voice with a lower resonance, from a slower talking person with a fluctuation and varied tone.

REGULATING SPEECH AND TONE

If you listen to yourself on the test recording or recorded sales call and find that your tone is in a higher register, practice dropping the tone a little lower by relaxing your voice, and lower the volume at which you are speaking.

Practice talking in a lower tone all the time, each time you speak, on socials calls, talking to friends and just in general.

I've been in the voice-over business for 20 years and had to learn to drop my voice considerably in order to become a saleable commodity to my VO agent when presenting me to potential clients. Several clients have told me after a sale that one of the reasons they bought from me was, that they just liked the sound of my voice. Not that you have to be a trained voice-over actor to make sales, but a pleasing sounding voice will add to your presentation, and at least it can't hurt.

ENERGY

If you have ever gone through a sales training class as a new hire, you've heard the phrase "Energy is contagious" many times. Yes it is, and you can believe it.

If you're excited about something, that excitement comes across to your potential client or customer, and suddenly they feel all "Jump'in up and down" about the product. Suddenly then they are asking buying questions like, "How much does it cost, do you have it in xxx colors." That's why there are salespeople, TO SELL, and enthusiasm along with energy are the two elements that sell products or services, they are the "Sizzle" on the steak. Once you get the prospective customer or client "Smelling" the sizzle, closing the deal is a "By-product" of that attitude, and it has the same effect on everyone around you.

***SMILING**

Why do you think almost every **radio** commercial is so upbeat, the people sound so positive, and cheerful? ANSWER: THEY'RE SMILING when they talk. You SEE it every time you watch a TV commercial, and they do the same thing on radio. Make a note to have a friend do this test with you. Close your eyes, and have them read a short paragraph or sentence off of a page of written material. The first time just read it straight, with no added color. The second time have them read it with a big smile on their face, and if you cannot tell which one is which, throw this book in the trash, because NOTHING is going to help you!

You can always tell if a person is smiling when they talk to you on the phone. It may not be like a flashing neon sign, but there is just something about that person and their voice that makes you feel upbeat, positive, and puts you in a good mood. Then ask yourself the question, "Which person is more effective in selling a product, a person in a good mood, not so good, neutral, or bad mood? Once again if you can't answer that last question...trash the book and get a job flipping burgers! I have people tell me that they were having a bad day, nothing was going right, and after talking to me for a while, they "Got happy."

Once again the type of energy you put out is the type of energy you get back, and who wouldn't want to buy something from someone who just made them feel better, happier, and more productive.

Zig Zigler, the famous motivational/sales guru once said, *"You never get what you want out of life, until you help enough people get what THEY want."* I believe that, and so should you! Help them get what they want, if they don't know, show them what they want and why.

HAPPINESS RULE: *You are not happy because your world is right, your world is right because you are happy.* (PsycoCybernetics) Be happy and things go your way, and vs/versa.
The more people you make happy, the more sales you will make. This is not rocket science people, JUST DO IT!

THE ART OF CONVERSATION
What is conversation anyway? Usually it's people talking, and many times never saying anything, or

anything for which you find worthwhile. These people who talk with no content or very little meaning to their speech are called BORING! They cause people around them to start looking at their watch, crossing and uncrossing their legs, looking out the window, and wondering what they're going to do for dinner that night. I'm sure you've encountered many of these types, and maybe even been one your self. So ask yourself, DO people start looking at their watches when I'm talking, etc.? If so, you may want to sharpen your conversation skills, because when you start to sell using the phone, you will realize very quickly the length of someone's attention span is very short, and gets shorter the longer you have them on the phone. It's up to you to become interesting to them, give them some "Audio candy", keep them wanting to hear more of YOUR conversation. How do we do this? See below.

RULES OF CONVERSATION IN SELLING

1. Courtesy:

It doesn't matter if you are in a face-to-face selling situation or using the telephone, the rule is the same:
NEVER talk ***over*** someone. Which is to say if they are talking, don't start talking before they stop talking. Also, if they do that to you, and talk over you, LET THEM!

Remember, you are the controller, but you must let them think THEY are in control. You regain control by interjecting a *QUESTION,* even a short, 3 or 4 word question. This means the person has to stop, consider and answer, and people like it when you seek their counsel, or want information from them. It makes them feel important, useful and once again makes them FEEL GOOD. One of your purposes in life (if you expect to get paid) as a salesperson it to: MAKE THEM FEEL GOOD! JUST DO IT!

2. PAUSE

Let a short pause come at the end of *their* spoken word BEFORE you start speaking. This shows them you value their info, and may be considering what they just said. This shows respect for their ideas, and gives weight to what you have to say next. If you start your next sentence with, "Hmmm", that really says you are considering what they just told you, and now they feel like you are really listening to them. This is a powerful rapport gaining technique that NOBODY ever uses, so the effect is gigantic!

3. FOCUSED SPEECH

Stay on the subject. People don't like it when you deviate off the subject at hand, plus they can get lost if they think you're talking about one thing and suddenly switch to another topic or subject.

4. BE BREIF BUT NOT SHORT

Keep your sentences a reasonable length, with out rambling on and on in a never ending out spewing of words. If you don't pause every so often you don't even know if the customer is still on the line. They might have gotten tired of your rambling and went to the bathroom or are off the phone.

5. CHECK THEIR "TEMPERATURE"

Always ask a question periodically to get their feedback on the big picture of "Are you still with me". I once was talking to this prospective client from one of the southern states, and I was rattling off a whole bunch of useless verbiage for about 3 minutes, and finally I said, "So all we need is to have FedEx come by and pick up your check, which is better morning or afternoon." The line is silent for a few seconds and he says, in this southern drawl, "DO WAT NIAAYNOOOWWW." He didn't hear a thing I said, had no idea of what the program was about that I was pitching, and it was my fault that he didn't, because I didn't check his presence on the line to see if he was actually with me, as a listener or a MIA (missing in action) causality.

6. LISTEN TO THE BACKGROUND

This will tell you a lot about your customer or potential client, and if it's a good time to be talking to them. What do you hear, baby crying (tells you where THEIR money's going), dog barking? It's probably some at the door or some other distraction. If there is a lot of noise, distractions, or they cannot hear you it's an important thing to ask, "I can hear that you're pretty busy right now, can I give you a call back later". This also qualifies them as to their level of interest in what you are selling. Some people can never just say, "NO I'm not interested." They will let you go through your entire pitch and then tell you, "Yeah but I don't have no money." The background noise can give you a wealth of information on where they live, how they live, and what things they are likely to feel positive about. If you hear music in the background, what is it, classical, country, jazz, wrap? This will tell you a lot about their personal tastes, and therein more about how to gain some degree of rapport with them. Obviously if you hear Prelude in E-Minor by Chopin, in the background you're not going to talk about how great a wrapper Ice Cube is and can he/she dig it? That's just one more tip on getting rapport. JUST DO IT.

7. NOTICE THEIR VOCABULARY

If you were selling a high-ticket item, IPO, or business opportunity with a considerable outlay, you'd like to know if a person has the money to spend. Even if you're not selling a super expensive product or service, it's still good to know if they have any expendable cash.

A person's vocabulary tells a lot about their lifestyle, station in life, level of intelligence and just who they are in general. If they use double negatives in a sentence, like, "I don't got no problem giv'in you the money right now", and your minimum buy-in is 20K, I would have some serious reservations on just how soon they would be sending me a check. It's obvious they've probably not graduated Magnum cum Laude from Yale, or maybe never graduated from anywhere.

But still, as they say, "Never pre-judge a client", it's just taking in the available information to give you a better picture of the customer. Every scrap of information you can get from and about them gives you more "Ammunition" and a better sighting device for your "Sales pistol". The more bullets in your "Gun" the better chance you have at bringing home the "Bacon."

COLD CALLING – WARMING IT UP

Probably the most disliked, frustrating, and avoided task in sales is cold calling. More than 60% of the numbers you dial are belong to someone that hates salespeople, don't want to be bothered, don't want what you're selling, and don't have the money anyway. Of the other 40% of the numbers dialed, the people on the other end will not meet the qualifications to become a client/customer after you begin to qualify them. Now you are down to a final 20% of "Possible" individuals that MAY become a deal, if they are still interested when they hear all the details of what their money will buy them. Then it is IF you've got a "Bring back" policy, IF their spouse or some other validating voice will condone the purchase, and a whole lot of other "If's" that only they can dream up.

The main point to stress here is that this is a COLD call. What are the characteristics of a cold call?

- The recipient is not expecting your call.
- The recipient most likely has zero interest in what you're selling.
- The recipient is not the right person to talk to or the wrong number anyway.

- The recipient cannot talk to you at the time.
- The recipient doesn't speak your language.
- You get a message machine*.
- The recipient has died.
- The recipient has bad health, can't talk to you.
- 10 other reasons that you will find if you do it long enough.

So how do you break through this wall of resistance, and indifference? You do something that separates the money makers from the hourly wage earners. You keep dialing! Now if you are at a job where there is a predictive dialer, and all you have to do is sit there and wait until you get a screen pop (name on your computer screen) then you will talk to many more people, but for now let's just pretend you have to do the dialing manually.

DIALING TIP:

Put your fingers on the key pads of the phone, with your middle finger on the pad for the number 5. You will feel a small bump or raised area on that one key. This is so you can FEEL the 5 key. Now make sure your other two fingers lie on either side of the 5 key touching the #4 and #6 key. Instead of hitting the numbers to be dialed with one finger in the "Hunt a peck" style, use all three fingers to dial the number. In starting out, you would want to look at the key pad as you dial, but it won't be long before you can dial the numbers WITHOUT looking at the phone. It doesn't take a genius to imagine where the ONE key is from the 5 key, then the TWO key is right next to it, and so on. You may as well dial the phone like this, because it doesn't take any more effort and in a week of "Dialing by feel" you will be twice as fast, and this will result in calling more leads, and talking to more people, which results in making more sales. By now you've figured out, this cold calling business is just a numbers game, and the more people you talk to, the more sales you will have.

HELLO – FIRST CONTACT

On a cold call the very first words out of your mouth should sound warm and friendly, like you already know the person, but not so common place as to cross the line of "Stupid". When someone does something that takes them outside the "Envelope" of reality, or common sense, that's STUPID. In this case we are talking about a level of being familiar with this person. Eventually they are going to find out that you're a salesperson, trying to make some kind of commission or get some kind of benefit from your call to them. Now they realize that you've "Tricked" them into thinking about you in a way that is not true, which really brings out the COLD in the cold call. DON'T DO IT.

SMILE (Again)
It is also good to keep a smile on your face as you are talking to this person, because anyone can tell when you're smiling as you talk. It doesn't take a psychologist to realize this, so use it all the time. Some people keep a mirror on their desk so they can SEE if they're smiling. This is a great idea, and a smile on your face does something else

VERY important. It puts YOU into a more positive STATE, and you can never be too positive, or too happy. This positive state carries through in everything you do, every call you make and the way you relate to everyone around you. It can even change the attitude you have if it's not as positive as you would like it to be at the time.

VALIDATION OF INFORMATION

There many times when you THINK you have a sale, it went very smoothly and you got the credit card or payment information easily, maybe you got it TOO easily. Going back to an earlier section, about the "***Time waster***", you may have gotten someone who just loves to "Jerk your chain", waste your time, and gets off on having you think you're a great salesperson, and in the end gives you a wrong address, credit card number or return contact info. There ARE people like this that have nothing better to do but string you along, and then pull the rug out from under you. To prevent this if things seem to happen too easily, (they say yes to everything without any questions or needing more info) you should really test their credibility. You can do this in several ways. Repeat back to them the credit card number, the entire address, or contact information...*INCORRECTLY*! If they don't correct you, then you know you have a time waster, chain yanker, or someone you should hang up on immediately. If you really think they just a space case and ARE a deal, give them YOUR number and tell them to call back because you've go to take another call etc. If they call back they just may be a deal but have no attention to detail.

CHAPTER 8
10 DOs & Don'ts FOR THE PHONE

In every sales position I have ever worked, every phone room I've ever set foot in, there have been people who constantly make mistakes that cost them the sale, turn the customer off, and end up with the salesperson giving them their phone number "In case" they want to call back to buy whatever is being sold. They broke one or more of these 10 rules.

People WANT to be sold on a deeper level, and when you do certain things or when you DO NOT do certain things you lessen your chance for closing the deal, making the sale and the customer saying they have to "Think about it". Which by the way is the proverbial "Kiss of death" for the sales person, because it's not saying no, it's not saying yes, and it's putting the sales situation into kind of a "Limbo" state of being. It simply means, or should mean to the salesperson that their customer/client is not convinced, has reservations they have not revealed, and needs to be "Re-pitched" and then a second (or third) closing attempt should be employed, which we will go over in later chapter.

If you fail to follow the "Rules" below, then in every sense of the word you have "Shot yourself in the foot", to employ the phrase people use when they want to illustrate someone doing something intentionally stupid, wrong, self-defeating, and I'm sure you can think up loads of

additional euphemisms.
There are several main concepts to keep in mind when presenting your product or service so as not to sabotage the presentation on your own or as we say "Shoot yourself in the foot."

1. NEVER, and I mean never, repeat back to the person the reason they just gave you for not buying.

Why is this so bad? First of all, they are telling you a "Reason" they don't want to buy. When you repeat that reason back to them now they've heard it once, from THEIR own lips, and once from YOURS, and you're the person who is trying to convince them to buy the product/service.

You just gave them a reason NOT to buy, and it's the *second* time they've heard it! Their subconscious mind is now programmed **2 times**, with negative information, half of which the customer did, and the other half of what YOU just said in repeating the reason they gave you. This should come under the category of "DUH" as far as lack of common sense that even the newest "Newby" salesperson should figure out by themselves. However, they never do and keep doing it every day, and can't understand why they never get any sales when encountering the first "No" or resistance.

Even experience salespeople do it, because they were not prepared for that type of objection, or that level of resistance, and they just don't know what to say, so they repeat back the last objection. This is obviously a poor attempt at preventing dead air, or silence. Many salespeople think this is a bad thing, so they just "Parrot" back the last phrase they hear the customer say, so as to give them time to think of what to say in rebuttal...*BAD IDEA*!

If the customer has got any smarts at all, they're thinking that you're some kind of mental retard, don't know what you're talking about, and start looking at their watch or making an excuse to get off the phone just to terminate the conversation. There are plenty of responses you can come up with that would be 100% better than repeating back their objection and you should pre-formulate those responses before the objection comes up. For example: Can't buy, I don't have the money right now". Response: "What happened, did your wife/husband max out your credit card"? ANYTHING but repeating what they just said. You just need to create the situation that gives you a second attempt at closing them. One direction you always take when someone says NO, is being in total agreement with them.

Example: "Sure I understand, you're in the same boat as most people / I was a while back / you're like my father/mother/friend had the same problem.

2. NEVER EVER TAKE LESS THAN 3 "NOs"

Did you ever hear the statement about a salesman's job? The first thing I learned about selling, either in person or over the phone was, "Your job doesn't start until your customer/client says NO! Up until that time you are nothing more than an order taker, and they make less than dishwashers.

One of my sales mentors used to preach, "If you don't make at least 3 people per hour hang up on you, you're not doing your job". All that means is close, present again, close, present again (from different angle) close, drop close, ask how you can get their business, close again, by this time if they haven't hung up, close again.

3. 4 THINGS TO A 2ND & 3RD CLOSE

1.ACKNOWLEDGE, "Yes I understand.
2.AGREE, "I've been in the same boat"
3.REDIRECT "This is how I handled.
4.SOLUTION "Let's do this...

This disarms them, makes them think the closing attempts are over and now they can relax. Now you can start the re-presentation/closing process all over again, but knowing at least one of their objections and how to deal with it or overcome it immediately.

4. NEVER LET ANYONE TELL YOU WHAT TO DO.

That is the first pit fall of loosing control of the sales situation. Ex: "I can't talk right now, call me back later." They don't give a fart in a tornado if you call them back, it just sounds good, and they think YOU think they'll be a sale, or at least more receptive when you call back. The truth is they'll never answer the phone, or have your number blocked. YOUR RESPONSE: Sure-be-glad-to-but, I won't be able to give you this one time/one call price on the xxx, if you don't take it while I'm on the call. Or: "I'm sorry but we're on a dialing machine and we can't call out, this is just a one time opportunity to buy, AND...I can give you this xxx along with the deal if you buy now...etc. It doesn't matter WHAT their reason for not talking, buying, listening, just go right ahead and pitch them like they were the best possible buyer in the world!

Now this sounds goods, and you start the phone call with the idea that you are going to employ this strategy, and maintain control, but something happens when they try to command you. You go DITHS (Deer in the headlights syndrome) and are all "Ah, er, well I ah, we ah, duh" and so forth. How do you prevent DITHS (deer in the headlights syndrome)? Pick a phrase or word to shout out to interrupt them, like "I CAN'T" or, "I CAN'T CALL OUT", or, "its A ONE TIME DEAL!!" This does 2 things, one, it breaks the command mode they are trying to put themselves in, and 2; it prevents you from succumbing to DITHS.

CLOSER'S AXIOM: *You can't say the wrong thing to the right person, and you can't say the right thing to the wrong person.*

Meaning, if they are the "Right" person, by the fact that they are interested, motivated, and have the money, even if you stumble over your presentation, don't come off as a genius, there is a good chance that they will still buy. By the same token if they don't want it, need it, don't have the

money, NOTHING you say will result in a sale. So if you have to stand on your head and spit wooden nickels to get their attention, go on to someone else!
If they are a deal, they WILL talk to you, if they're not, nothing you can say will make them want to buy, and quit wasting your time.

5. NEVER ASK A PERSON IF THEY *WANT* TO BUY.

Just ASSUME they want to buy what you're selling. Ex: "Would you be interested in taking advantage of this offer Mr. Jones?" If they say yes, they know they're committing to the deal, and they never want to say yes to a salesman! They might as well sell themselves, what do they need you for? Just ask a closing type of question that would *suggest* they would be saying yes to the deal by answering the question at all. Ex: "So I just need a Visa or MC, which one is best for you right now"? Or, "We have delivery times of Monday and Tuesday in the afternoon, which is better for you", or, "How many of those units would you like today?"

6. NEVER USE CONTRACTIONS

Words like can't, don't, won't, doesn't, haven't, shouldn't, isn't, and the like. If you never use these then your pitch will become a lot more positive, and your response to their objections, will also become more positive. On another positive note, you can not repeat back to them their negative reason (as mentioned earlier) which was the reason they said they are not going to buy, if you do not use a contraction like "Can't, won't, shouldn't, doesn't, isn't", because that is probably exactly what they said when giving you that negative reason for not buying.

7. NEVER GET IN AN ARGUMENT

Someone may say something totally opposite to what you believe, what you think, how you view something, but as far as you're concerned, they are ALWAYS right. Use phrases like, "Ya know I'm the same way myself". Or, "Ya know what; you and I are a lot alike". Don't take the opportunity to expose someone's lack of knowledge, because you know so much more. You may win the argument, but most likely you'll lose the sale, and guess what, you're the one that will be eating beans for the next few days instead of steak. It's your job as a successful sales person to make your potential client or customer feel like they are smarter, quicker, more intelligent, and better versed in every way THAN YOU ARE! This elevates their level of comfort, and it's much easier to sell somebody something when they FEEL comfortable, than when they're not. When they feel like they are the more informed, or "Smarter" one in the sales situation it gives them a greater feeling of confidence, and makes them *think* they are in control.

So if you use a lower profile of knowledge, experience, and let them take the lead, if they happen to be that type or person, (if they happen to be that leader type) then you will get a lot farther, and most likely end up getting the sale when it's all said and done.

8. NEVER USE BAD GRAMMER

Bad grammar or improper language is a deal killer, especially if you are dealing with people who have some degree of academic background, college, or schooling past high school. It labels you as being on the lower rung of intelligence, a high school dropout, and just plain uneducated. Examples would be using a double negative phrase like: "I ain't got no problem in sending you some of our information". This is a real buzz-kill for most potential customers/clients, because they like to think that they are dealing with an individual that is intelligent, and this is not his or her first job in the work force. They want someone they can communicate with on a one to one level, and will convey information properly to them in the sales situation. Along those lines it is also a major mistake to use profanity, racial or sexual connotations or slurs in the course of your sales presentation anywhere any time.

9. NEVER TALK PAST THE SALE

Once in a while you will actually get someone who knows all about what you are selling, has researched it, is pre-sold on the idea of buying it and WANTS IT! This is great, but some salespeople feel they've to keep plodding along with their pitch and "Double sell" it.

Or they just might talk right by the "Yes I want it" commitment by the buyer and keep on jabbering along like they never heard them say, "I'll take it." Finally the customer thinks, "There must be something wrong with this product/service, because this salesperson keeps trying to shove it off on me when I just said I want it." Then turns around and walks off, or if on the phone, hangs up.

If/when, someone says they want it, asks the price, you tell them the price, then they say "OK"...that's it, STOP!

Your next words out of your mouth should be, "Let me get your method of payment, and we're all set". Some salespeople are so "Flabbergasted" when they get a positive response to the close they don't know what to do.

In this case just treat the customer as if it happens all the time, each day, every day, and they are just one of many. This is a good time to ask for a referral, and now you've got another good potential sale.

Whatever you do, DO NOT TRY TO UPSELL or tack anything else on the deal UNTIL you get payment for THIS sale or deal. Later on you can mention that up sell or better advantage of buying more quantity etc. but GET THE PAYMENT NOW!

10. NEVER TALK PAST THE CLOSE

What is talking past the close? That is when the client/customer says, "Ok, we'll take the blue one." And you say, "Oh I thought you liked the red one." with this statement you ignored the "WE'LL TAKE THE... xxx one. WRONG! Your response in that case would be..."GREAT! Good choice I'll write it up."

When you deliver your close after a presentation you need to structure it so it becomes a yes or no answer, or one that just by answering at all, means they want to buy it.

At any rate when you come to the end of the close and it's, "Can I write this one up for 'ya?" SHUT UP! You've heard it 100 times if you've been in any kind of sales training – THE NEXT PERSON WHO TALKS LOSES. Don't let it be you. That's "Talking past the close." NEVER do it!

I once let a customer sit for 2 minuets on the phone without saying a word after I asked for the sale. I thought he might have hung up, but the line never went dead, so I knew he was still there.

As it turns out, he was actually playing the "Who talks next, loses", game with me. Finally after the dead silence, he says, "OK write it up", and that was that.

SUBTLE BUYING SIGNS

Too many salespeople, or people who TRY to sell things, never pick up on the subtle under the table conversations someone has with themselves or a couple together.

A quick shift of the eyes locking together if a couple, is usually look of agreement, it's just that you have to figure out if the agreement is positive or negative. Usually a smile will mean a positive perception on a product or service, and a wrinkled brow, or stretched lips, bitten edge of the lip,

kissing the air with puckered lips, none of these are great buying signs. You never know with a client/customer when the "I've got to have it" impulse kicks in, but if you don't recognize it when it does, you stand to be put on the "Back burner" of importance, by that person, because, you just talked past the close.
Now your client/customer is thinking, "What do I have to do, hit this guy over the head with the contract?"

CHAPTER 9
FACE-TO-FACE SELLING

There are people who are good at some things and not so good at others. There are people who lend themselves to FTF selling better than on the phone, and they like to get away from the office, get outside, and it gives them a great cense of freedom by not being chained to a desk or shackled to a phone in a stuffy office. If you're one of those then you know who you are, what you are good at, and you probably don't try to be someone you're not. If you like FTF selling then you realize it's an entire different situation that any other method of selling. In some ways it's better than selling on the phone and some ways it's worse. On the phone your appearance is not important; in person you must present a visual image that is pleasing, or one that puts the customer at ease. This image has also got to present to the customer/client the fact that you know what you're doing or talking about. Ex: if you were selling backhoes or semi-trailer trucks you wouldn't approach a potential client wearing a suit and tie. A pair of blue jeans, and cowboy boots would get you a lot further. So let's get into the VISUAL side of FTF selling and examine what works.

DRESS FOR SUCCESS

That is the title of a book somewhere, look it up if you want, but how you dress when you are meeting a potential client for the first time is one of the most important aspects of the sales cycle. If you keep in mind you are trying to impress upon someone that you are good at what you do, knowledgeable in that you know the product or services, and that you are not on a rung on the ladder of life somewhere so high above them that they can't even see the tops of your shoes.

The bottom line is, if you could be their mirror image with the same type of dress, degree of formal attire, or informal, they will think, "He/she looks just like me", and who wouldn't want to buy something from themselves? We'll go into this a little later, but the idea here is to look like, sound like, talk like, and act like your customer. It's called mirroring, matching & pacing (see Chap. 5)

We are going to break it down to three sections to make it easy to understand.

APPEARANCE – Clothes

How you look to some people carries more influence that anything else you can say or do, because it's the first time they have any information on who you or before you say a word. So let's take what you wear and analyze how it affects the outcome of sale or no sale.

COLORS

The colors you choose have a great affect on people, and many studies have been done to prove it. So, let's look at color and see how it all works.

BLUE: It is no accident that every commercial

you see on TV selling something that needs credibility like a car dealer, doctor, lawyer etc., they have a BLUE shirt, blue suit, and I'm surprised they don't get the "BLUE MAN GROUP" to do the advertisement. Blue conveys feelings like "True blue", credibility, truth, trust, loyalty, wisdom, and a peaceful surrounding. This is exactly the type of feelings you want to be portraying in your interview. Blue is a calming color (ocean and sky) and sends out a signal to the client that you are indeed honest and sincere. Studies have shown that wearing the color blue to a client meeting will increase your chances of getting the sale rather than wearing any other color.

RED: In contrast to the color blue, the color red stirs emotions more than any other color. The color red is a strong color, very emotional, an extreme color that in a sales situation can work against you. Unlike blue which has a calming effect, the color red is a fiery color and can be an intimidating color projecting you as a controller, power monger, just wanting your commission, and willing to say anything to get it. NEVER wear red if you want to win a new client over. Now on the other hand if you are going into a negation, and want to exude power, and strength, a red tie would be in order.

GREY: Grey gives the look of sophistication and authority. In a corporate environment the color grey is professional and portrays an individual as being confident without being intimidating. It would be appropriate for the person in management, or authority in nature.

COMBINATIONS: A light blue shirt with a dark blue pattern tie for men would be good. Even a red, white and blue stripped tie says, patriotic, trustworthy, and "Made in America". For women a dark to medium blue pants suit or skirt, with a grey to maroon scarf over a white blouse would be impressive.

For men as far as shirts and ties, the old tried and true rule of prints and plains still holds true. Plain shirt - print tie / print shirt - plain tie. NEVER break this rule, unless you want to look like an "Engineer", and they have absolutely no clue on how to dress. Just because a T.V. announcer does it doesn't make it right, or keep it from looking like a bunch of rusty wires in front of a corduroy blanket!

APPEARANCE:

GROOMING & ACCESSORIES

Remembering the rule: Look like your client, you need to consider your grooming. This means hair, mustache (if present), fingernails, and incidentals.

CORPORATE LOOK

HAIR: Haircut, is it the type of cut you think your client has, does it fit the look you want to convey. In the corporate world the look is short to medium, and somewhat conservative.

Fingernails: Clean and possibly manicured

Shoes: Shined and possibly wingtips

Socks: Dark and longer with stretch tops to keep them up.

Belt: Smaller buckle, no flashy or bronc rider's

champion award buckle here.
Glasses if needed: Small frameless
Watch: If you got a Rolex, wear it if you're meeting a higher level client with a high-ticket sale. If you are meeting a lower level person with a lesser dollar value sale, DON'T wear it. You don't want to look like you make more money than your client/customer, or getting rich off of his or her sale.
Pen: If you got a $600 Mont Blanc wear it, but the same rule above applies.

Portfolio: Leather bound notebook, take it.

SNAPPY CASUAL LOOK
Your hair, your clothes, your grooming is "Whatever" just don't look TOO good or too much better that your potential client. Leave the expensive jewelry at home; you don't want to make this person think they're financing your extravagant life style. A nice pair of slacks and collared shirt is appropriate.

SKATEBOARDER/SURFER LOOK
If you're selling surfboards, skateboards, or you're a computer geek it's a very different wild and whacko look. Bottom line, nobody cares, wear whatever you want.

1st FACE-TO-FACE MEETING
Naturally the first meeting is the most important "Image creator", this is the meeting that will create the client's opinion of you and be hard to change. Here is when we learn to MATCH, MIRROR AND PACE (we'll go over it again). This

technique is much easier in person than on the phone so make sure to use these techniques. It doesn't matter if it's in a corporate boardroom or a pool room, the technique is the same.

MIRRORING:

This is a technique that is very easy to learn, but harder to remember to DO. It's very simple; however the customer/client sits stands or occupies space, you adopt a mirrored image. Which ever hand they have on the table, you match it (as in a mirror). Which ever leg they cross, do the same thing, if it's a hand in a pocket, do the same thing, same side. You BECOME the other person as if they would be looking in a mirror.

MATCHING:

This technique is exactly as it sounds, you match everything about them, their speech, their walk, their gestures, everything. If they talk fast, so do you, if they slow their speech, so do you, and if you can, blink at the same rate per minute as they, this will gain you instant rapport.

EYE BLINKS PER MINUTE

Now this is an almost impossible task to do while carrying on an intelligent conversation, because it requires your conscious mind to be thinking of 3 things at the same time. These are, their blinks per minute, what they are saying, and how you will respond to what has been said. That's a tall order, which takes a lot of practice, but it can be done, and produces INSTANT rapport or link up with someone. I wouldn't recommend trying it for the first time with a new or important client, so practice it first with friend or new acquaintances. If done incorrectly or at the wrong pace it can have a negative effect on someone. I knew a guy who sent Morse code in the military, and he would "Blink" you his conversation in Morse code as he talked (even when you told him not to do it) so I know it can be done in matching someone. He of course drove people crazy, and you may also if you try it. You may also miss some important info or clues to buying signs. So practice this on friends, and practice a LOT before trying on a client or customer.

BREATHING

If you watch someone's diaphragm and breath at the same rate that they are breathing, you will gain instant rapport with them. Another difficult skill to learn because, once again, it requires conscious thought in several areas while carrying on a conversation and making some sense out of that conversation. Try it in practice with friends first before using it on a major account executive.

PACING:

This technique is where you draw THEM over to YOUR level of being. After you match and mirror them you begin to change the pace (speed up or slow down) and see if they come with you. It's a clear indication of gaining rapport with them, and it lets you know they are coming along with you. Now you have "PACED" them and can begin to "Reprogram" their inner computer or belief system in order to get the responses you want.

These are the FTF techniques you can employ to gain rapport with a potential client or customer, and it makes selling them a product that they happen to have SOME degree of interest in, much easier. The main idea here is to gain a level of trust and rapport with your customer, with this level of trust you can guide the customer toward a level of product or service that you feel would be most beneficial for their needs. In the end they will be more satisfied because they confided in you the exact item, for the exact price they could afford and in the end, got exactly what they wanted. Which is the salesman's book of accomplishments is the "Brass ring" of sales. A satisfied customer that got what they not only needed but also wanted at the same time, all because the way you treated them, sold them and followed up on making sure they got what they wanted and what they needed. That's called customer satisfaction, and it's a rare commodity in today's marketplace.

CHAPTER 10
NON-VERBAL TECHNIQUES

Every day when we communicate with other people, 80 to 90% of how we communicate is NON-VERBAL. This means it is at a SUB-conscious level, or below the level of normal consciousness. Which in simpler terms means, we don't KNOW we are taking the information in at the time. However; after it is in our subconscious mind it begins to filter up to our conscious mind and the information begins to take shape, and we start to make decisions based on this filtering process.

In the previous chapter you learned about mirroring, matching and pacing, now we are going to go into more detail about those non-verbal techniques. We are going to explore *WHEN* the client/customer is accessing their mental computer, *where* in their little world of mental file cabinets do they put their "Good" information of things they like, and where they put the negative information of things they don't like. Along with that, how to capitalize on the "Good" areas and stay away from the "Bad" areas, when you finally know where they are.

MATCHING

This as explained before, is simply matching a person's behavior, stance, and a little bit more. Essentially you look at someone's over all behavior, and after a few minutes you can get an overall picture of their behavior patterns. Examples would be, are they high energy, fidgety, how much time do they spend actually looking AT you while talking TO you.

EYE CONTACT:

There are people who cannot hear you unless they are looking AT you. Then there are people who can never hear, or absorb what you are saying unless they are NOT looking at you. This is a very important trait to notice and pick up on, if it is a glaring personality trait. If they constantly make eye contact with you, you do the same. If the opposite is true, adopt THAT personality trait.

Where are their hands all the time? Are their hands moving, waving around, in their pockets, at their side, do they use gestures like pointing, holding up the amount of fingers to illustrate a number. When they hold out their hands to make a point are the palms up or down, do they inspect their finger nails when talking, all these things give you insight as to their personality, and who they are. After you notice these behavioral traits, you begin to match them, stand like they stand, regulate our hand motions and patters like they do, you actually BECOME them while you are together.

In a short time they begin to feel more at ease with you because you remind them of THEM. Now you're getting what you call rapport, and the better you are at getting rapport, quicker you gain their confidence, the more open and friendly they become. Now, who would not want to buy something from a friend?

Now you have only one problem. You don't want to become TOO friendly, because someone can always say no to a friend much easier that to a closer type salesman. So, there is this fine line of being friendly without becoming their bosom Buddy. They still need (and usually want) a closer salesman/woman with a command presence SELL them the deal in manner that says, "How can you say no to this!" and assume the sale is a done deal.

THE SALESMAN'S NOD

Nodding your head up and down is the universal signal for YES. This is something you may have heard about, and it's still a great non-verbal technique. A technique that no matter what someone says about how trite it is, how overused it is, and how everybody knows all about it...it still works. First of all we are referring to an "In person" face to face meeting with your customer/client where they can see you.

As you are talking to them about your product or service, your head will nod up and down periodically at different times. This is especially effective when you want to deliver a fact, or important phrase to your sales prospect, and have it remembered, or conveyed in a very positive manner.

It can also be done at the exact second you want to add weight to certain words.

Example: "Mr. Jones, you'll find out very soon that we have the ***VERY (nod) BEST (nod)*** service department in the city."

This sends a non-verbal message to that person's inner or subconscious mind that they have received some very positive information, and that this info is important for them to remember.

HANDS SAY IT ALL

Just for fun, when you are at a party or interacting with people in any way, notice what they do with their hands while they are talking. Almost all of the people you will come in contact with are going to be doing something with their hands as they talk, like waving all around trying to describe and event or happening, or showing you how big or small something is or was.

If they make a gesture with the palm up, it's a good bet that they are a more open person, willing to share their thoughts, and opinions easily, and without reservation. This type person is usually more trustworthy, tells it like it is, and more openly honest with most of their dealings.

This is not to say a person is less trustworthy or honest if gesturing with the palms down, it just may mean they are a little more guarded, and not as open, and free spirited.

If a person is always fidgeting with their jewelry like their wedding or class ring, it may mean they are a little apprehensive about the moment or situation at hand, and may need a little more reassurance.

TAP TAP TAP

If you want to "Mark" a certain word to stand out

in a person's subconscious mind or linger in their memory (which adds a ton of credibility and importance) all you have to do is add an accompanying sound along with it. That's why when a car salesman taps the hood of a car he is presenting to someone at the exact second he says a certain word, he is illustrating that word to be more important to the meaning of the phrase or sentence he just uttered.

Example: "Mr. Jones, this is the ***BEST*** (tap) ***BUY*** (tap) of any car on our lot. And ***BUY*** (tap) ***NOW*** (tap) I think ***YOU*** (TAP) ***LIKE ME*** (TAP TAP) realize the reliability of this make and model as something that would be ***SAFE*** (tap) and ***PROTECTIVE*** (tap) for you and your family."

He has just "Subconsciously" marked the words **BEST BUY – BUY NOW - YOU LIKE ME- and SAFE & PROTECTIVE.**

Suddenly that customer is going to get a message from their subconscious filtered up to their conscious mind in a form of wanting to "Buy the car now, they like the salesman, and it's safe and protective", and they don't know exactly WHY they think this way, they just know they do.

OPEN ARMS

A good salesperson should always try to be as open and transparent with their customer/clients as possible. A good way to make sure this is illustrated while in their presence is to be very careful of your hands arms. NEVER fold your arms over your chest in front of your client/customer. It is a piece of defensive behavior that should be eliminated from all your actions. If you don't know what to do with your hands, clasp them BEHIND your back. Now your front is totally open which says that you're totally open too. This will go a long way with gaining trust and rapport with a new customer/client.

LEAN IN

If you want to give more meaning to a phrase or word, as you deliver it, lean toward your customer, not too much, don't get in their face, but just a little closer is good. It makes them feel like you're sharing something "Secret" and of great value with them that no one else knows, or is suppose to know. This once again gains rapport and credibility, and you can never have too much of that.

CHAPTER 11
LISTENING

Have you ever met someone who by their obvious behavior and body language, does not listen? How about a person who only seems to be listening so they know when it is their turn to speak, or starts speaking before you're finished talking? How does that make you feel? Frustrated. Angered. Maybe disheartened that your words are not valued. The quote above reinforces the notion that listening to someone is really the highest form of flattery. When we listen, not only do we hear, but we also build relationships with those who we are listening to. We are telling them that they are important to us and that we care about what they have to say. This leads to friendships.

IMPORTANCE OF LISTENING

Almost everyone would agree that the most important skill in sales is, communication with the customer. In sales this communication cannot just be one-sided; it needs to be a give and take relationship. As a salesperson, we need to be able to understand what the customer's needs and wants are – therefore we ask them questions. But only when we LISTEN and tune into their answers are we able to translate what they say into information that can help us provide them a solution.
In sales we listen to:

1) Gain valuable information to uncover clues

about possible solutions to meet a customer's wants and needs.
2) Emphasize with the customer to better match the solution to their lifestyle and wants.

3) Demonstrate respect for the customer, making them feel good about the sales interaction and relationship that is being developed.

If we put it another way, listening can be broken down into two basic functions.

FUNCTION 1: RECEPTION

Reception is the act of hearing and receiving the message from the speaker. This is the first sensory stage of listening. If you're not concentrating on the speaker and have your mind somewhere else, the incoming messages are not clear, and you have a very skewed view of what has been said, let alone know how appropriately respond to it. This is called POOR LISTENING!

FUNCTION 2: DECIPHERING

This is HOW our brain makes sense (to us and sometimes only us) and interprets the message that was heard to begin with. As humans we eventually learn to associate words with meanings. That's why when we hear a foreign language we are not familiar with; we cannot understand the words or their meaning. Words can potentially have different meanings to different people as in the fun party example of the game called Rumor. Some tells a short story to the person next to them and that person relates it to the person next to them and so on around the room. By the time it gets back to the original teller of the story it sounds nothing like the original tale.

It is in this stage of listening that the poor listener fills in his or her own "Blanks" of what we don't understand or can't comprehend. Instead of asking the speaker, "What did you just say", we allow them to continue babbling on and on and pretty soon we're totally lost or make up our own description of what we THOUGHT we heard.

BEING AN ATTENTIVE LISTENER

It is important to understand the different tactics you can employ to become a better listener. Question-based selling engages the customer by listening to them - helping you tune-in to their needs, which eventually leads to the sale.

Here are some crucial tips to listening more effectively.

TAKE DETAILED NOTES

How much can the average person remember? Have you ever been out dining with a company of friends at a restaurant and the waitress fails to write down your order? How many times does your meal come out perfectly with no errors? Or do you have to do a plate exchange after they've left or remind them who got what?

Unfortunately the human memory has its limitations. While it is easier to remember vague concepts or events – it's much harder to recall small details during conversation. In selling – the money is in the details. We need to be able to match the customer's stated needs and wants back to a solution we can provide. But in order to do this effectively – we need to be able to recall ALL stated needs and wants and use the customer's words in our recommendations.

AVOID PASSIVE LISTENING

Passive listening does not require any engagement. Instead the listener will hear and maybe absorb, but will not acknowledge, nor provide any feedback on what is being said. This is the closest form of listening to one-way communication.

Passive listeners are most in danger of being distracted by other happenings in our environment. These distractions may lead to missing important information and confusion around what is being told. If the passive listener is the salesperson – most likely they will fail at recommending the right product because they cannot tie it back to the customer's needs. If the passive listener is the customer – salespeople will usually end up feature dumping, leading to dead-end selling presentation because the customer's needs were never discovered.

IT'S NOT ABOUT YOU!

Finding the right solution for your customer is your #1 priority. It's not about what you want to sell them. Nor is it about trying to look impressive

by showing off your product knowledge. As a great salesperson you need to put all personal agendas and bias aside, so that you can clear your mind and fully tune-in to your customer's needs.
After asking a question you NEVER want to interrupt; instead shut up and let them fully answer what you asked. Do not anticipate what to say next or feel you are smart enough to know what they will say next. Do not interject a story about yourself. Do not make faces at something that you do not agree with. Simply do not move on until you have fully listened to the customer's response. If you do not, you risk prejudging the customer and inhibiting the customer's train of thought.

Listening and Multi-Tasking Equal TROUBLE!
When listening to a customer remove any obstructions that might stand in your way. The customer should always have your undivided attention. Do not try to do multiple activities when listening to a customer. Customers are able to recognize those salespeople who are "pretending" to listen. Not only will this send the wrong message to the customer, but also this will result in misunderstanding and missed information.

When you engage a customer drop everything you're doing. Avoid being preoccupied with anything else. Show them they are most important to you and open both ears.

ACKNOWLEDGE & CONNECT

As salespeople – it is important that we provide the customer with signs of recognition; that we have heard and understood what they were saying. We can accomplish this by displaying subtle visual or audio cues throughout the conversation and in our body language. Some examples of these cues may be:

VISUAL: Nodding, Smiling, Leaning in towards the Customer, Writing what they are saying, Constant Eye Contact

AUDIO: Saying things like, "Yes", "uh-huh", "Right", "I understand", anything to let the speaker know you are receiving, and *understanding* what he/she is saying. These cues demonstrate your listening ability. Customers who feel that you are listening and care about what they say will most likely speak longer and give you the information you need to help them provide a solution to their problem, or get them into the right product or service.

LISTENING FOR MORE THAN WORDS

Would you like to know more about your potential client/customer, and gain insight into their world and or environment? Then start listening to the sounds around them when they are on the phone. Is there a baby crying a foot away from the phone? If so it means the person is holding a child and probably has all their attention on that child.

In so doing, is not in any way absorbing *ANYTHING* you're saying, let alone going to be giving you a payment right then for whatever your selling. Ask to call back at a better time. Is there a dog barking all the time? It could mean someone is at the door, which is a sale killer immediately. Ask if you can call back at a better time. Is there a T.V. or radio blasting away, which means this person could be hard of hearing, or they feel the T.V., radio, or video game is more important. You need to control the sales situation by asking them to turn down this distraction so you can hear them. If they choose not to do so, it's a clear indication that they are not controllable, and probably not a good candidate for a possible sale. Listen to their breathing, is it labored, sporadic or regular. This may indicate a health condition you should be aware of, especially if you are selling a health related service or product. Are there sounds of traffic in the background? If so ask if they are driving, and ask if it is alright to be talking with them at that time.

If they are driving, (on a cell phone) it's a sure bet their attention is not totally on you and what you are telling them, and at the close they'll tell you they have to call you back for payment, which most likely will NEVER happen. All of the above are part of the sophisticated level of listening, and once again, *Good salesmen are great talkers, but great salesmen are good listeners*.

CHAPTER 12
SETPS OF THE SALE - OLD VS NEW

If you remember a few years back what it was like selling any product or service, the main sections could be divided into basically 3 main areas. 1. Gaining rapport 2. The presentation, and 3. Closing. If you put it in a pictorial graph representing the time spent in each section it would look something like the illustration below.

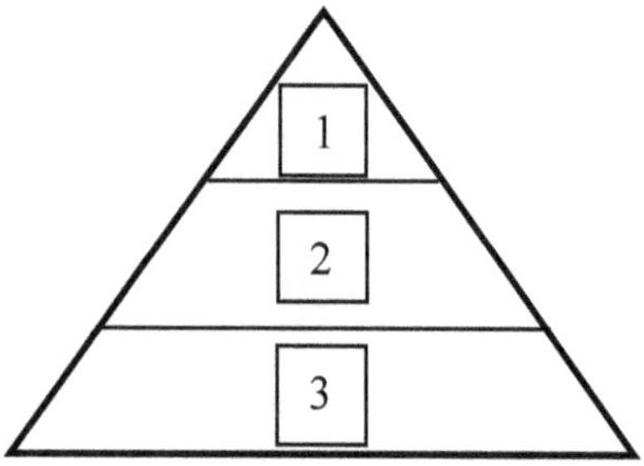

1. Gaining rapport: Not a lot of time was spent here in the initial stages of client relationship. It was, "Hello, how 'Ya doing, how can I help you, what are you looking for", etc. The salesperson never got to learn too much about the client/customer, never got to truly understand his/her inner needs, and probably didn't really care in the first place. Unknowingly the salesperson was just groping around the deep dark reaches of what the customer really wanted and probably wasted a lot of time showing them something that was not even close to what they wanted or even needed.

2. Presentation: The display of the product/service with the explanation of all the benefits, how much the customer/client will love and use the product or service. This takes a set amount of time, is carefully arranged and orchestrated and rarely changes. The time spent here does depend on customer interest, knowledge, level of customer input and participation. There is also a level of product/service complexity to consider, but in general the time spent was considerably more that than section one.

3. Closing: This is where most of the time was spent with the customer/client, because it came down to that person making a buying decision or rejecting the product/service. If the initial response was negative then the salesperson (if they are a closer type) would always keep the line of communication going, by asking if there was anything the customer/client needed to know, anything that was omitted from the presentation that may clarify the benefits, etc., and any other excuse the salesperson could think of to just keep the sales situation alive, and get another chance at, once again closing the sale. This is the method of selling the way it USE to be, but things have changed drastically in the field of sales, and the art of closing business. Through exhaustive psychological research of human behavior, interaction, and a whole lot of other testing and focus groups, a new "Phoenix" has arisen from the ashes of the people who have crashed and burned in their failed attempts at selling their STUFF! We now have found out more about how

people "Process" the incoming information they receive, how it controls their inner or subconscious mind, and what actually triggers that magical signal to BUY!

EMOTION

So what's the bottom line here? What *does* trigger that signal to buy when there was no or little interest present initially? When there was resistance at the start of the closing attempt, what changed that buyers mind, what turned things around for the closer? People with a whole lot more knowledge, research, and what they consider as "Facts" can argue (and will) about the answer to that question until the end of time. They will say things like "Benefits tell, stories sell", and go on an on about what a super salesman is, and how they work wonders with customers, but when it's all said and done, there's one answer that everyone agrees upon, to some degree. That answer is...EMOTION. A person will buy something they don't need; with money they can't (or are not suppose to) spend, in order to have something that they have a strong EMOTION or feeling about. When the salesperson has gotten the message from the buyer that there is this strong level of emotion or attraction to the product or service, and then if the salesperson has done their job at making the customer/client feel comfortable and "Safe" about the buying situation, there is a good or even great chance for a sale, and everybody's happy.

So now how does the sales person bring the client to that place of feeling "Safe" and comfortable, so

that the "Buy now" signal doesn't get hung up or re-directed to the outer cosmos of Xanadue when it was just ready to be transmitted to the conscience mind?
There is this little concept called RAPPORT, which we mentioned earlier. Before feeling comfortable with the product, the client/customer has got to become comfortable with the salesperson. In order to make someone feel comfortable with you, or around you, it is necessary to get a level of rapport with them. In case you missed or skipped over the section on rapport earlier, you should turn back to that section and re-read it, because that is what everything hinges on in creating a level of comfort in your client/customer.

So let's take a minute and examine what the word comfortable actually means in this context. One way you can define comfortable is to describe the WAY you feel when you ARE comfortable. How does that feel? A great way of describing a difficult concept or abstract meaning is to sometimes describe what it is NOT. In this case when you feel comfortable there is no tension in or around you. You feel at ease, the environment you are in is tension free, and that makes you feel comfortable. The salesperson is NOT expecting anything from you. You have no responsibility, and you don't have to worry about having to come up with a reason to be shopping, or looking for something, the act of which will create a sales situation that you will have to figure out how to say "NO" to a salesperson asking you to buy. This is comfort at it's finest state for the buyer.

Now that you are re-introduced to the concept of rapport, let's talk about a new concept of selling that makes a lot more sense, and brings about a higher level of success in closed business for the salesperson. This new slant on selling, works in all sales situations whether you are face-to-face, on the telephone, or even in written correspondence. Let's take that pyramid of time spent on the 3 sections of the sales situation, and turn it upside down, but with the numbers remaining in the same positions. It would look like this illustration that follows.

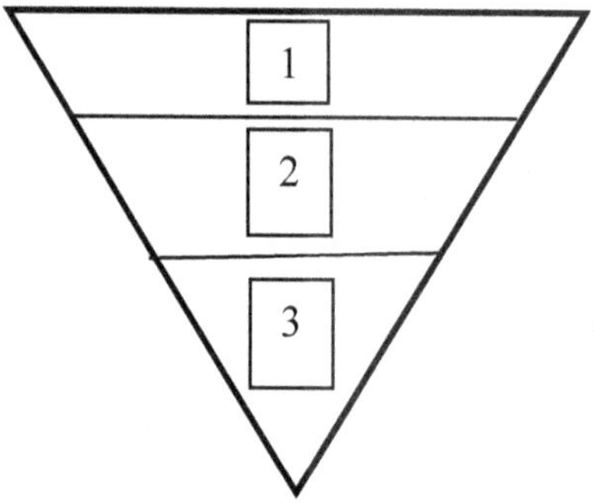

The numbers correspond to the same values (1=Rapport, 2=Presentation, 3=closing)
Here we can see that there is a major amount of time in gaining rapport with the client/customer. A good example would be if you would be selling appliances in a major chain home store. Someone is going to possibly spend hundreds, if not thousands of dollars on a major refrigerator, or washer/dryer etc., and they want the best dollar value for the money. At the time they are just comparing products and prices. Car sales is another venue where this inverted pyramid

becomes very important. The client/customer must feel comfortable with the entire process and it starts with the salesperson.
Some one said, "Make a friend, make a sale", and I strongly disagree with that statement. I don't disagree with the fact that nobody is going to buy something from someone they don't like, but it's really easy to tell a friend "NO" in a closing attempt when trying to sell any product or service. People buy from a command type of personality, or a leader type of individual. If they are not a leader, or commander, they buy form a person that they would like to BE like. People like to be SOLD, and they like to be LED, and guided through the sales situation. This is where the rapport section of the sales situation comes in. The true definition of rapport is when someone THINKS you care more about THEIR satisfaction, well-being, and comfort that making a sale. Rapport is when the client/customer perceives you as a person who is a lot like them in your mannerisms, desires, goals, and aspirations. How could a person just like them LIE to you? How could a person just like them be untruthful, or devious? Once you've achieved that level of communication and "Link up" with someone, you've achieved RAPPORT.

As in the pyramid example, if you spend more time on gaining rapport, you will spend LESS time on closing. In fact, they will already be PRE-closed when you get to that point because they TRUST you, believe in you and what you say about your product, how it performs, and or service.

CHAPTER 13
PROSPECTING FOR LEADS

How would you like to sell snow to an Eskimo, steak to a rancher, firewood to a tree removal service, and we could go on and on? The point is, in order to MAKE a sale you have to find someone who's in need of that product or service, to *some* degree.

That's where the art of prospecting comes to the foreground, and becomes one of your most important duties. Without leads of people who have a significant inclination toward what you're selling, you're dead in the water. It's true you have to do a little work on creating the desire, and product glorification portion of the equation. The initial call to the person you think needs what you've got, is the first step in the selling process, or they could just pick up the phone after seeing your ad for XXX and order it, or some of it, or ALL of it. That's why we have the definition of an order taker (which is at one level) and a salesperson (at a higher level), and a master closer at still a higher level. They make totally different amounts of money with totally different levels of expenditure, effort, and responsibility.

The first consideration of prospecting is to consider the perfect profile of the person to which you would like to pitch your service or product. Make a list of all the main characteristics, personality traits, and mannerisms of that person. Some of these on the list might be, their age, job classification, IQ, family life and background. Write down any thing you can think of that would describe this perfect person who would want your service or product. Then make a time table of what their hours of work or non-work hours would be and the best time to call them.

Most sales organizations have already done this for you to maximize your efforts in finding the right people to talk to, because the more money YOU make, the more money THEY make. However; if you are on your own in developing a sales force, or just you crusading out there, you need to develop your efforts to this level of focus. Otherwise you'll spend a huge amount of wasted time calling/contacting the wrong people at the wrong time, and burn out quicker than a paper match in a hurricane.

Now that you know all about your potential client/customer, and when they can be contacted for the highest capture rate of success in calling or contacting, START CALLING/CONTACTING.

TIME MANAGEMENT

Time is one of the most important things we never get back once it has passed. There are no "Time machines" that can take us back to a previous event, and allow us to change the outcome, or alter that event. That's in the movies, and certainly been explored, and hypothesized upon over and over again, which kind of makes you want to go back in time and burn the movie scripts/film reels of that very subject.

So, when you view TIME as a very precious commodity, and realize the implications of what happens in the NOW, and how it affects the future, you begin to get the idea of how important YOUR time is when deciding to spend that time or put it toward and endeavor. With that in mind let us explore some of the critical areas of time management and see how we can better use this very illusive and precious thing we call TIME.

YOUR ROAD or TIME MAP

In every endeavor, you've got to have a plan of action, a clear picture of the end result (if you don't know where you're going how do you know when you get there), and how are you going to accomplish these goals. So, let's examine a road map to success with the emphasis on TIME spent. First of all you need to make an outline of the time you already HAVE available. Go through the mental scenario of your typical day, what you do, how you do it, and block out the available time you will allot for PROSPECTING. It may be different each day, the same every day, but this should be a clear and concise picture of what you do each week. This includes time of inactivity, recreation, and the work you want to accomplish. Once you have got this down on paper, you have a much clearer picture of TIME as it relates to YOU. When I talk to people about the time management principal, and making a "Time map", they look at me in a funny quizzical way, kind'a glance sideways at their co-workers, other people in the room, and I know they are asking themselves if hiring me to present a seminar or sales training session, was a good idea. I just say, "Just do it". Begrudgingly they comply, and half way through it or near the end you hear the moans and groans coming out. People are muttering under their breath, things like "This can't be real", or "I never realized I spent this amount of time showering", and a whole plethora of verbal realizations. People don't realize their every day habits because they are too close to the actual events. Can't see the "Forest for the trees" syndrome. When you start to write it down, make a chart, put it on paper, you begin to actually realize where you put this precious commodity called TIME. The first step in improving or changing something is to evaluate what you already HAVE or are doing, and then look at your evaluations in a very objective light. You may be quite surprised at where you spend your time, how you let it "Escape" from you without any real accomplishment.

Sure you need some down time, but it's always a good thing to realize how much of it is making up your waking hours. Sometimes you just want to sit down in a chair or by a window and think of nothing, and this is good. The trouble with down time or recreation time, you start enjoying it too much, and forget that "It's" controlling you, instead of the other way around. That's where the TIME MAP is so beneficial in showing you (without bias) where your time is being spent. This is, of course you ADHERE to your time map, and don't get distracted by things you'd rather do, places

you'd rather be or think about, and a host of other "Things". We all do it, but never forget the TIME AXIOM: Time well spent with yourself or a friend, brings satisfaction in all things".
The question here is, what is the definition of "Time well spent". You may have a definition of that phrase that means a special something to you, and it may mean stupidity to someone else, but if your time spent on a project, friend, partner, or endeavor brings you to a place of fulfillment, or great happiness...then it could be considered TIME WELL SPENT.

But let's keep talking about how time management relates to sales and making you more money, since that's why you probably bought this book.

Each day on your time map, have listed the amount of calls you want to place in order to achieve ONE SALE. That's it, one sale; let's not get KRA-ZIE here, just one sale. All you are searching for in this instance is what we call, "Little victories", and before long you *WILL* have your little victory of contacting just the right person, who is in just the right frame of mind and may even say, "Ya know I'M really glad you called me 'cause I been want'n one of those xxx you been sell'in."

That's the call you would have missed if you'd gone home at 5:00...because...it was 5:00 and EVERYBODY knows that quitting time is 5:00 pm! As soon as you learn that a killer salesperson does not live by the clock, you're on your way to making that $50 and hour or $100 and hour that you heard people do make in the sales arena. Time management can be THE most important commodity you can manage, and guess what, it is YOURS. Nobody can take it from you; nobody can tell you you're a loser for working too many hours, or working too hard. They can only be jealous of you and your new Corvette or Mercedes, because THEY went home at 5:00! Don't think about it...JUST DO IT!

CHAPTER 14
MAINTAINING CONTROL

In every sales situation maintaining control over the conversation, the sales environment, and people involved, is very important. The big question is, how do you do this without appearing like the German Gestapo, and coming off looking like a whip cracking over-lord? This is achieved by a thing called diplomacy, and tactfulness. Politicians have mastered this over the years and that's why they have been so successful in getting elected. If you notice when asked almost any kind of a question that will declare their "Bias" or stand on a subject, they will go into a treatise of all kinds of information and at the end you're still asking yourself, "What was the question to begin with?" They never gave up CONTROL in the verbal exchange of information, because they never did actually ANSEWER the question directly.

Which brings us to one of the most powerful tools of maintaining control in any verbal exchange, and it can be summed up with one word...QUESTIONS.

SALEMANS AXIOM: Questions are answers, and gain control.

If you want to control a conversation, change the direction of where a conversation is going, and redirect the focus or subject of interaction, ASK A QUESTION!

First of all, it forces someone to stop in their "Verbal tracks" and give you an answer. In order to do this, they have to temporarily give up control of the conversation, shift gears, and now you have control, or at least more control. It also shows them that you are interested in them and what they think, which helps in gaining rapport with them.

Secondly, if the question well thought out before asking, the answer should substantiate the point YOU are trying to make, and give you a broader vision of what's going on in the other person's mind or point of view. Now with this new vision or perspective, you can formulate a much better response to that person's resistance to your closing attempt.

There is always this "Back & forth" tug-of-war in a sales situation with both parties, and you must be careful not to tug too hard, knowing if you win the contest you may lose the sale. Never forget who has the check book or credit card, and who can walk away without using either one.

If you can maintain control of the conversation as well as the overall sales situation without making this obvious, you stand a much better chance of seeing that credit card or check book in the end. You may even have to give up a little of that control to get the sale, it's much like having to let out a little line (let 'em run) when trying to catch bigger fish than your line is designed to hold.

Remember, it's not whether you win or lose the

debate, but does the customer/client feel good about saying, "YES"! The yes means you get paid, and you're happy, the customer/client is happy, your boss is happy, and everyone on down the line is...HAPPY!

So isn't that funny? If you start out happy, that's' usually the way you end up at the end of the sales presentation, HAPPY!

CONTROLLING THE SALES ENVIRONMENT

When we talk about control we need to think about CHANNELING the energy we have to deal with rather that meeting it head on. One way to channel this energy is to control the one thing we CAN have control over, and that's the environment we find ourselves in during the sales situation. It can be broken down into two areas, YOUR area, and THEIR area.

1. *YOUR* SALES ENVIRONMENT

This is where people come to YOU as potential customers/clients. You have a storefront operation, or office etc. It has to be as distraction free as possible. This is sometimes very difficult, if not impossible to achieve but you need to do your best to remove as many distractions as you can. If it's a retail establishment, then that comes under the heading of impossible to control distractions, but you should try to provide as much private area as you can to make it so.

Car dealerships have cubicles for their

salespeople, banks have individual desks for their customer service techs, and there is usually a way you can configure your place to achieve some degree of privacy for your customer/clients. You want them to be able to focus on just you, what you are telling them and be able to hear their responses clearly and without interruption. This gives them the opportunity to consider your presentation, along with the price, and other options in a manner to make an informed decision without any undue pressure, and distractions. If necessary put your phone on call forwarding to a message machine, or your cell phone on vibrate so as not to break the "Ready to buy" mood, as soon as you finally attain that state of being. When the customer/client finally gets in the reverie of potentially owning or buying the product at hand, you don't want some jangling phone jumping off the hook or crying baby howling to break the mood and cause them to ask themselves, "Whoa just a minute here, let me think about this for a while, maybe come back TOMORROW!"

GROUP PRESENTATIONS

Now here is a situation where you *really* have to control the immediate sales environment. You've got a group of people sitting or standing around talking, and interacting, and you've got to get their attention off of whatever conversations they've gotten into, and start paying attention to you. So, they need minimal distractions, comfortable environment, and you've got to grab their attention immediately.

LATE ARRIVALS:
If there is a specific time for the presentation, make sure that after a certain time no more people are admitted to the presentation. Lock the door or put a sign on it saying that the presentation time is now past and they will have to come back later. This is important for several reasons. One, is that people coming in late disturb not only the people who are there on time, trying to absorb what you are saying, buy disturb YOU in your effective presentation, and flow of information. They also will miss portions of the presentation that may make the difference in them buying or not buying, not to mention asking "Already answered" questions.

TOO EARLY
Just as bad as being late, is too early, because now they sit there and try to pick your brains for information on the service or product you are presenting, and you have to fend off questions about how everything will be covered in the presentation...when it starts.

I presented a sales pitch for a social club, and would lock the door that had a sign on it that said, "Meeting starts at 7 pm sharp". People who got there early would have to wait outside until I opened the door at promptly 7 pm. It saved me a lot of time making "Mini presentations" to everyone who got there a half hour early.

APPEARANCE
Have the presentation room free of "Junk", or a

cluttered desk, and overflowing trash cans etc. The more orderly your environment appears, the more professional YOU appear.
Try to give the environment an "Appropriate" appearance, meaning if you're a travel agency have exotic travel photos on the wall, if a social organization have shots of happy people interacting having a great time. Whatever says, "This is my business" in wall treatment.

Just try to control your sales environment as much as you can to insure the best chance for a distraction free sales situation. If you need to have sales aids or support information, make sure it is where you can retrieve it easily, and efficiently. This in itself makes you look commanding and in control, and people buy from a commanding presence or personality. They want to be lead by a "Leader", and it's hard to look like a leader when you can't even find your calculator or xxx.

2. *THEIR* SALES ENVIRONMENT

This is the other element of control you need to deal with in order to give yourself the best chance of success in getting that "Yes, I'll take it" response from your customer/client.

In this case you are going into THEIR home or office either by phone or in person, and it's much more difficult to control this type of sales situation. You can't just tell someone what to do in their own home, or office. You can make suggestions like "Is it possible you can let your

dog outside while we're talking so I can better show you the finer points of this xxxx. Or "I think it would be better if I came back at a time when you didn't have company or xxx going on to divide your attention, because it is very important we get all this information correct" etc. etc. This is a subtle way of controlling the sales environment in a way to not be offensive to your customer or potential client.
Unless you have their undivided attention you're basically beat before you start, and there's nothing worse that a "Half-presentation" to turn a customer off. It can make them feel like they have enough information to make a buying decision *without* you being present, after they've thought about it. You want to BE the reason they may their buying decision. YOU should decide when then buy, not them deciding when they by. Otherwise why have a salesperson at all, you could just put the product or service out there and say, "Here it is, sign up, buy it, pay for it if you want, when you want, and thanks a lot."

To control their environment you can feign things like not being able to hear them if they are on a speakerphone, or if the TV is too loud (*NEVER* pitch someone with a television on AT ALL) in the background. That's a clear sign they're not listening to you or only partly listening. Unless they can hear you perfectly there is very little chance they are going to be persuaded to buy anything from a telemarketer.

DINNER TIME

If it's dinner time, now you've got your work cut out for you and you may a well schedule a better time for a call back, because nobody cares about you or the "Thing" you're selling when they're just about to have dinner.
One guy says to me, "Oh I never talk to anyone around dinner time, call back later." I want to say, "Hey you idiot, you left me a message saying your home was going to be foreclosed upon in 20 days and you'd rather eat dinner instead of find out how to prevent losing your home?" People's value system is sometimes very skewed in a strange and destructive direction.

But once again, he's the one with the check book and or the credit card, and the ability to say, "OK, here's the CC number to get me started.

So, as much as I'd like to try to control HIS environment, and tell him to skip dinner for 15 minutes, and listen to what I had to say, so he can save his home (DUH). I can't do that, and I would be as stupid as he was if I thought I'm was ever going to sign up a new client, when there is this type of distraction in the sales situation. As an end result I just schedule a better time to call and talk to this person.

Always remember one fact of successful selling: PEOPLE *DO NOT BUY FROM SOMEONE WHO TICKS THEM OFF!*

Which leads us to the next very closely related chapter.

CHAPTER 15
IRON HAND–VELVET GLOVE

That oxymoron describes the attributes of the master closer to a tee. He is very firm with his customer/client, but makes that firmness feel good in a way that gives the person a feeling of confidence, and well being.
You know all the parameters you must stay within as far as price, terms, service, guarantee, delivery, and other specific areas of the deal. Every potential client/customer will try to push you to the very end of your "Envelope of profitability", and then some. It is your job to use an "Iron hand" when it comes to bending these rules of acceptance. At the same time, you need to make the customer realize that you are thinking only of his/her well being and best interests, along with fulfilling the needs about which they just finished telling you, and wanting the best for them in general.

This is especially important in dealing with people on the phone, with profit making commodities like stocks, precious metals, investments, intellectual properties, real estate, automobile sales, and most high ticket items.

Politicians have developed this skill to a fine art. They are the most tactful speakers in the Universe. Someone said that a if a political candidate is any good he is the kind of person that, after listening to your side of the story, or pitch...can tell you to "Go to hell" in a way that

will make you anticipate arriving!
Having the "Iron hand" of adhering to price constraints, and company parameters, unless it's offset by the "Velvet glove" of empathy, and a caring spirit, which is a very difficult balancing act to pull off. Only the smoothest of master closers have learned how to do it automatically, that's why they're called "Master closers". They are the best at defining what a great salesperson is in every sense of the word. A great salesperson is someone who can make their product or service look, sound, and feel better that all the competition, *WITHOUT LYING!*

So, with every squeeze of this iron hand, you must make a few strokes on the customer/client with the velvet glove. You'll find that more people will say yes to you when you think they are not even close to making a decision in the positive direction of buying. This is because they not only respond to your firmness, but also to your compassion to their problems and difficulties.

CHAPTER 16
TIME MANAGEMENT & LIFE'S BALANCE

When you think of the balancing act that most of us go through just to maintain "Level", (not being sucked into the storm drain of Life) it's pretty awesome, and more so to some than others. Take the single mom who has an 8 to 5 job, and at least one unruly kid that wants a new pair of Michael Jordan $125 super basketball sneakers so he can keep up with the rest of the cell phone toting, Air Jordan wearing other 8th graders. Or the father with 5 kids who's moonlighting as a cab driver at night right after he gets off his shoe salesman's job.

There is the college student who is taking too many hours so that is makes him late for his job at the hamburger joint where he's working to pay for the extra hours of courses he's taking in the first place.

Does the phrase "Balancing act" ring any bells for 'ya? You probably are doing some kind of a balancing act with your life right now, and that's why you're read this. Meaning, if this sounds like anything close to your situation, then this chapter is for you. Read it slowly in a quiet room with a highlighter in your hand, and with no one around.

To define balance is to say that there is never too much of anything in one area of your life. That covers a whole lot of ground, and who is to say what is "Too much", and right now you're probably thinking "I wish I had some say in this equation, because if I did, I'd probably have that balance". Most of the time people feel like they are going over Niagara Falls in a barrel as far as having control over *anything*, let alone balance in their life.

When you think about it, you DO have more of a say in that department of balance. It's called "Time management", and most of us would think if we had time to take a time management course, we'd have time to manage thinking about managing our time.

At some point in our lives everybody gets to the point of feeling like a "One arm paper hanger", and it doesn't matter how well we manage our time, there's just not enough of it. That's when you discover the most important thing about time; there's never enough of it, and once it's gone, it's gone.

So now let's talk about balance with that "Time thing" in mind, and the older you get the more important that time thing becomes. Get out a paper / pencil (God should be the only one who uses a pen) and write down 3 things that are most important to you, or do it below, and how much time you spend on each one. If you need more space than 2 lines because there are more than 2 things that are that important, then write them down also, somewhere else on another sheet of paper if necessary.

1.____
____

2.____

3.____
____

Now that you've got this little picture of what your existing time is filled with, ask yourself if the time you have allotted is really enough or too much for that actual activity. You've probably thought about this time relationship, but putting it on paper is the best way to view it in a very statistical light and actually think about it in terms you can relate to. Ask yourself things like "How much time do I spend with my kids actually listening to them, how much time do I spend fixing things I screw up". Someone said that many people spend half their life making mistakes and the other half regretting them.

One of the purposes of this chapter is to get you to take a better, closer, LOOK at what you're doing, how you're doing it, and then what you can to do to change it or make it better. Again, time management will always give you a better balance in your life. It will provide at least a road map of how to get somewhere you've wanted to go, and know when you actually arrive. The problem is, even though we have a map, sometimes we don't use it. We think we can find an easier, better way to get where we want to go (if you actually know where that is) and we get off the map to cut corners. While we're talking about cutting corners, sometimes you'll find the corner you cut off, so to speak, has the information on it that you'll need in the future, which would have saved you...TIME. As the saying goes, "Be careful of the toes you step on today, because they may be connected to the ass you have to kiss tomorrow!"

Now, back to the balance of your life, and let's examine how you might have gotten to the place of "No time" in the first place.

1. You said, "Yes" to too many people, because you can't say no to anyone.
This is a common occurrence in a lot of well meaning people. They probably feel that somewhere along the line they "Owe" somebody or some group or the cosmos out there somewhere, something that they need to pay back somehow. They become a "Doormat" cleaning everyone's shoes that gets near them, and they have never learned to "Just say no". That's called "Self-assertion", when you say NO.
Take closer evaluation of your priorities, and evaluate each request with the idea that BALANCE is the important thing here realizing that instead of a NO for an answer, maybe "Don't even think about it" would be a better reply. Take control, or at least "More" control, and you will get better balance. JUST DO IT!

2. When you did say "Yes" to a commitment, did you have a clear understanding of what exactly was expected of you, and the time it will take to

cover that "Yes". Many people who want your time only tell you half of the story, or not exactly what is involved until you get deeper into your commitment, and then they unload the "Oh by the way I forgot to tell you about this little extra little dipsydoddel thing we do every Monday, Wednesday, and Friday, you can handle that can't you?" Now you have the RIGHT to say..."Don't even think about it."

3. You enjoy too many things at once. This gets so many people into an "Imbalance crunch" that they find very difficult to escape. They like to sample life's "Goodness" from lots of different areas of life, and before they know it, they need to take a vacation, to go on vacation. A friend of mine calls me up from Maui Hi., while I'm working on my house in Illinois in November and it's cold, I'm digging a ditch for a pipeline into the house. He says, "I'm so depressed, I don't know whether to go surfing today or ride my motorcycle to the other side of the island to see my girlfriend, I just don't have enough time anymore". I hung up on him!

4. Passion: You start liking one thing so much that you forget everything else. THIS can really cause an imbalance quickly. Sure, be passionate about your pursuits, but remember the balancing act. Too much of a good thing is a bad thing. The trouble is, how do you know when you've had too much of a good thing until once again, you're on that flaming skateboard of life, flying down hill into a lake of gasoline! DON'T DO IT!

5. You had too many Margaritas (or whatevers) and made a promise (or promises)that sounded good at the time. There's an appropriate Jimmy Buffett song called "A permanent reminder of a temporary feeling". It's about a guy who gets a tattoo when he's drunk. It's still there for the rest of his life. It's about a girl that gets pregnant; the "Reminder" is there for life. This is how we get an imbalance of too many commitments / not enough time. YOU - WERE - NOT - THINKING! 5 seconds of thought can prevent 5 years of regret...or more.

Permanent Reminder Axiom:
LIFE IS NOT A VIDEO TAPE, THERE IS NO REWIND, NO REPLAY!

There are loads of people that you can see every day that are carrying around a *"Permanent reminder of a temporary feeling"*. Some of those specific things are:

- Tattoos
- A Baby
- Missing fingers
- A cast on their body
- A wedding ring

I'm sure you can think of many others, but the point is, mistakes in life come to everyone, it's just that some people become "Mistake magnets", by the choices they make. Don't be standing too close to one of these types in an electrical storm, or in a bar at closing time. Lightning comes in different forms, sizes, and shapes. You don't need a permanent reminder.

Balance in life is a skill few people ever learn. The trick is to learn when you're out of balance while you can still "Get it back". Notice if you're always in a hurry, if you drive too fast to get where you are going because you're always late. Are you always tired in the morning because of saying up too late trying to "Catch up?" Is it hard to get to sleep at night because you're always thinking of what you need to do the next day? On "Life's telephone" do you always have someone on "Hold" while talking to some else? Do you keep thinking, "I need to take a vacation"?

These are signs that you need to slow down, and gain that balance back, so quit thinking about it and...JUST DO IT.

CHAPTER 17
APPOINTMENTS & GETTING THEM

When you think about appointments, you need to consider the surrounding data, reasons, and implications of getting this appointment. First of all, HOW is the appointment made, by phone or in person. Let's take the appointment made by phone first of all. What are the surrounding factors of getting an appointment with someone to make a pitch or show them your product for the first time without previously meeting them directly?

First things first, you need to talk DIRECTLY with the person in question. Most of the time they have this "Wall" around them. This wall is invariably the "Gate keeper". It is this person's sole job in life to make sure that their boss, manager, husband, wife, or whoever you want to talk to...NEVER has to talk to a salesperson, or anyone else they don't want to talk with.

There are many ways to circumvent the gate keeper so let's examine the alternatives.
1. Pretend you're an old friend. You can do this by only using the potential client's first name in a manner that suggests you're more that just a salesperson with a sales pitch, trying to SELL something. Like, "Hi, I was try'n to get a hold of Jimmy...if he's around today". Without actually SAYING "He's my fishing/golfing/tennis/drink'inbuddy" or whatever. You have, by your casualness painted a picture of

PREVIOUS association with this person. One thing you CANNOT do is lie, and actually say, we've got a golf date tomorrow...we're old school mates, we're xxxx buddies. When he finds out who you are and what you actually want, he will be VERY put off, and you'll be lucky to have him give you the time of day for the rest of your life!

So, there is this fine line of trying to NOT sound like a salesperson without crossing the barrier of an outright lie.

Several ways of sounding like a friend instead of a salesperson.

1. Overall casual demeanor, using first names when asking for that person.

2. If you have their name saying things like, "He/She's the person I've dealing with on this matter".

3. Previous association: "I was just checking up on the info I sent him/her to see if they got it, are they available?".

4. If you have to answer the question, "Where are you calling from", just say half the name or an abbreviated part of the name. EX: Instead of saying "John Jones from Southland employment agency" , say, "It's John over at Southland."

Many times the decision maker tells his receptionist to NEVER let a salesman get through to him/her. If this is the case you can bank on the

fact you'll be screened very well and most likely have to "Leave a message".
Speaking of leaving messages, that's something you want to have well thought out, probably written down so you will be able to read it verbatim.

LEAVING MESSAGES

- It's very important to be able to leave the kind of message for someone that accomplishes the following parameters. It is very direct and coveys:
- Exactly why you are calling.
- States the reason for your call
- Tells exactly how you can help them
- Says where you got their info (if you can)
- States all your contact info
- Thanks them for their time

APPOINTMENT AXIOM: You can't *GET* an appointment if you can't *TALK* to that person directly. There may be exceptions to that rule, as in the case where the appointee will refer you to his secretary or assistant to make an appointment. However; this is just an extension of that person WANTING to see or talk to you as a result of hearing what you have to say to begin with in the first conversation.

When you do finally get that person on the line you can do one of two things in trying to arrange a time of meeting with them.

BEST
1.1. Depending on how much you think they want

to see you or speak with you again, YOU decided when the appointment will be. You tell them you have a xxx time available on xxx day or a different day/time, providing an optional appointment time, and ask which one will be more appropriate for them. That way you are holding the control of the situation and they are more likely to show up for the appointment.

GOOD
2. Give them several times to choose from, thereby suggesting that you're a busy person, your time is very valuable, and they should feel privileged to have that meeting.

WEAK
3. If they are pressed for time and give you the idea they will hang up any second, you ask THEM what would be good for their schedule. This is the weakest approach bordering on begging, but a meeting is a meeting. You should also take note that this kind of a potential meeting setup should be re-verified the morning of the meeting to make sure that person is going to be there.

MEETING / ATTENDANCE AXIOM: The amount of positive interest shown by your potential client/customer is in direct proportion to the chances of their attendance at your purposed meeting.

SINCERITY SIGNALS
When setting up a meeting with someone you need to listen carefully to the tone they take with you when agreeing to the meeting and

surrounding details. These signals are forecasting factors of how "Real" they are in their desire to meet with you, listen to your pitch, and degree of need as far as how important you or your product is to their situation.

GREAT TONE

If they sound egger to give you information, like the address, their cell phone number, the actual directions to the meeting spot, describe the building etc., then you can feel confident that you've got a solid agreement to meet.

JUST OK TONE

If it sounds like they are using a computer, typing, shuffling papers, talking to someone in the room, or dividing their attention between you and anything else, this is not good. You had better bring them back to your end of the phone or presence before you finalize the meeting, or you could be wasting your time. With this person, you should make sure to re-verify the meeting time/place, and details *before* leaving your location. Otherwise, you may be sitting at an empty table.

POOR TONE

If you have to "Pry" the information about the exact time, and place of the meeting from this person it should tell you immediately that you're dealing with someone with low level of interest in your product or service, and could care less about receiving or meeting you at the set time. If they are obviously busy while talking to you, distracted or there are sounds of "Action" going on all around them that would be distracting, just ask them if it's a bad time. Tell them you can see they are busy, and arrange to call them back later to set a firm time for a meeting. Anything more than that is a clear indication that you're wasting YOUR time and that is something that you never get back.

When you do get the meeting time make sure BOTH of you know exactly where, when, and all other parameters of the meeting place. Get the directions of the meeting spot, and repeat them.
Now that you have got the appointment, put all Goggle Maps, and reminders in place. Such as, on your GPS, cell phone, alarm watch, calendar, etc. Make sure to give yourself extra time to get there so when you turn the wrong way on the wrong street and end up in the wrong county, you'll still have time to make it.

Never forget YOU'RE the salesperson, and they can do business with any one of 10 people just like you and your company. With this thought in mind BE ON TIME OR EARLY. It's better to have you waiting on them than the other way around.

If you are early, explain to them that you were not sure what the traffic would be like, if it would take you more time than you thought to arrive, and not to think they need to meet with you early just because you're early. This lets them know you are thinking of THEIR time as very valuable, and have a very professional approach to business in general.

JUST DO IT!

CHAPTER 18
THE BUTTON UP

This is one thing that a lot of salespeople do not pay enough attention to, and it results in coming back to bite them in the aspects of the most inappropriate places, and at the worst times.

Let's break down the positive attributes of the complete and proper "Button up" by defining exactly what it is.

Button up: The actual meaning came from the military. If there was one button Unbuttoned on your uniform, be it combat or class A's, you were considered "Out of uniform", and needed to "Button up". Which in context means to have all items attended to and nothing left undone.

In sales, it means to finish up all the details TO THE CUSTOMER'S SATISFACTION, and thereby make the customer/client FEEL like they have done the right thing, made the right move, and came away with the best deal they could have negotiated. Unless the customer/client is "Buttoned up" properly and all questions answered to their satisfaction, they can have buyers remorse, need to "Think about it" before the grace period is over (if there is one). All in all the deal can go "South" on you if they don't feel good about the whole entire thing.

You need to go through the papers, contract, or agreement and go over all of the parameters of the sale including the exact price with all charges, tax, and duties included, and recap each and every aspect of the product about which they may have questions.

If all of this is done properly, they will have that "Good feeling" when they think about the deal you gave them, about the company you represent, and a positive feeling about YOU!

There is a saying in the sales business: A DEAL IS A DEAL IS A DEAL. Which means if a deal becomes, "Not a deal" it was never a deal in the first place. If you have to do a "Magnamous" job of convincing, selling, and overcoming loads of objections, verifying information, corroboration of facts...the chances of the deal going through are somewhat on the negative side. THIS is where the button up is VERY important. As mentioned previously the scenario of the "Sales box", it puts the customer in a position of HAVING to say "Yes". If you do a proper button up, that also creates a "Button up", box that prevents a deal from falling apart because the client/customer didn't "Understand" all of the ramifications of the deal, didn't "Realize" that certain facts were going to effect the end result, and just as a bottom line, "Wiggle out" of the deal.

Once again, if the client/customer has been properly prepared, you have gotten a better than reasonable amount of rapport with them, they will demonstrate a higher level of confidence in you and your company.

This level of confidence is the glue that holds a deal together if there are any gray areas in which the client is not totally comfortable.

So, don't be afraid to ask the client/customer all the questions to get all the objections out in the open. Make sure to let them know all the charges up front, and then ask them if there is anything they want clarified.

This will save you a lot of trouble, and enforce your credibility along with creating a lot more happy and satisfied customers, and these people will in turn recommend more client/customers to you. Which brings us to the next chapter...CUSTOMER SATISFACTION

CHAPTER 19
CUSTOMER SATISFACTION

It has been said that one "Opps" wipes out 10 "Attaboyz". Why is it that one molecule of negativity can contaminate and possibly destroy an entire universe of well being?

The "One bad apple" syndrome is always what people point out when ONE salesperson says ONE thing wrong or incorrectly. Just ONE little bitty smudge on a white shirt, or piece of lettuce on a grocery floor, and we get totally bummed out, totally dysfunctional, because people dwell on the negative view, more than the positive.

Why is this!?

If we had the answer to that, we would most likely have the answer to every other question that has been plaguing mankind since the Garden of Eden.

It seems that people in general find it harder to deal with, and react more powerfully to negative occurrences or being taken advantage of, than receiving good, and positive gifts, and treatment.

They seem to forget very quickly the great treatment they received at the car dealership when getting their oil changed, but remember, very well, the poor service they got two weeks ago in a fast food bar. So let's try and define what customer satisfaction actually is and how it is achieved.

CUSTOMER SATISFACTION: When the client/customer feels they have gotten exactly what they wanted, and maybe even a little more that they wanted for what they agreed to pay.

How can a client/customer NOT be satisfied when they get what is described above?

1. They think the salesperson SHOULD have sold them a different, better, bigger, smaller, more than, less than, other than...whatever they bought. It may have cost more, but saved them more in the long run and the salesperson should have been mindful of this and told them.

2. They got the best price on xxx but had to pay more shipping than another source they could have bought from.

3. They are just a complaining consumer who needs drama in their life and is NEVER satisfied with what they get from ANYONE.

THE CUSTOMER IS ALWAYS RIGHT

Now the person who coined that phrase must have had a REAL handle on how to make a customer satisfied!

Many people are just not satisfied unless they get to "Beat up" a salesperson to get what THEY think is the best deal they can get. It makes them feel like they've done their best, "Brought home the beacon, conquered the dragon, fought off the marauders", and defended the homeland.

Sadly enough when you take a closer look at these people you realize why they are this way and it would help to take note of their appearance/attitude so when you encounter another one of these types, you see the red flag waving above their head that says "PROBLEM PERSON".

Back to "The customer is always right" syndrome...it is your job as a salesperson to HELP them toward the decision to BUY. You do this by being friendly, asking questions about them to determine their needs, and it makes them feel like you care. It's always better if you DO care, because that's what makes good salespeople GREAT, not to mention the fact that most people can tell when you DON'T care, even if you are good at *pretending* to care.

One of these tasks in the "Helping to buy", category is to make them FEEL like they are better than they are, smarter than average buyer, more special than your "Regular" client/customers, and that you actually LIKE them as a person as well as a client/customer. Here are some ways to portray things to cause your client/customer to feel comfortable with you.

1. Honesty: This probably the most powerful of human traits, and easiest to repute. If you make a claim that is not true, it will sooner or later be discovered. D U H! Maybe the client/customer knows enough about the subject/product to realize you just lied. You're in...TROUBLE!

There goes your credibility, which incidentally is the other half of honesty. Once you are caught in a lie you only have 2 options.

1. You claim that you mis-spoke, you got confused and thought they were talking about xxx. Which is ANOTHER lie that they may know the answer to without the product instructional manual.

2. You just don't know enough about the product, but you didn't want to look too stupid in front of a new client/customer, so you dreamed up a xxx number or xxx claim to fill the silence instead of just saying, "I know the answer, but I'll find out for you."

OK, let's go back to the purpose of this book, to get you "MORE AND BETTER SALES" and the reason you're reading this, MORE MONEY!

Your credibility as a salesperson is one of your greatest assets. When people realize that what you say...you do, and the information you dispense is accurate, then these people begin to like you and will buy from you.

Credibility breeds trust, and if your client/customer trusts you to make the best decision, not based on price, then they will TRUST you and then they will buy from you, and tell all their friends to buy from you, and that means...MORE MONEY.

So, which came first the trust in you, or the YOU

that changed to become more trustworthy? The answer to that has got to be obvious, YOU have to have to change first, YOU have to take a closer look at how you view your client/customers and To become better at sales, unless you're the greatest salesperson that ever lived and really don't need this book...somewhere, somehow there has to be a change in the way people perceive you, and how you believe.

That change will bring a big difference in the amount of sales you turn in at the end of the day and the amount of people you help at the end of the month.

Concern yourself more with customer satisfaction than commissions paid, and you will most likely end up as top salesperson at the end of the month, and you know what that means? MORE MONEY!

What does that mean in general? Less pressure on you to EARN money, and now you are much less desperate to get that extra sale, you're not worried about LOSING that sale, and your entire demeanor changes. You feel more confident, people can tell, you don't NEED their money, you could care less if they buy, and this attitude is a terrific magnet to more sales and again...MORE MONEY! Of course you know what that means?

Now they're going to ask you to be the sales manager, train other people to do what you've learned how to do, and of course that means...MORE MONEY!

JUST DO IT!

CHAPTER 20
GOAL SETTING

Once again, if you don't know where you're going, how do you know when you get there?

Any great athlete, achiever, or successful salesperson has always known the value of setting goals as a way of giving the inner mind, or subconscious a vision of WHERE you want to go, where you want to end up, and a target at which to shoot.

If you were going to climb a mountain would you choose Mt. Everest as the first challenge to tackle? Of course not, so why do it with your sales efforts.

The best course of goal setting is to picture, or aim for an ATTAINABLE goal, one that is within reach of YOUR capabilities. Sure you can put a picture of a Bentley or Rolls Royce in front of your desk, but not unless you're CEO of IBM or Goggle. Start with a Toyota or a Corvette, in this case.

Pick a reasonable amount of calls to make each day, a reasonable amount of people to qualify as a good profile of a person/company to send an email or prospectus etc., and don't stop until you reach that number. Figure out how many of these contacts it takes to generate someone with the money...interest...and allows a certain degree of control (by you), and keep on the phone until you get there.

Suddenly your success rate will change, and there's nothing like success to attract more success.

JUST DO IT!

CHAPTER 21
EXCITEMENT & EMOTION

You've probably heard the phrase, "Sell the SIZZLE, and not just the steak". If you break the sales process down into just one thing what would that be? Ask yourself the big question, "What is the greatest motivator that causes people to reach for their wallet, pull out their credit card, dig deep for that cash wherever it may be?" There's been a ton of research done on what makes people buy something, and they always come up with basically the same answer...SIZZLE.

So, lets analyze sizzle, and see if we can find out what actually makes it "Siz". What we're really talking about in every case is a thing called EMOTION. People THINK about buying something because of NEED, but they "Pull the trigger" on buying because of emotion.

Why does someone buy something they don't need? They WANT IT, so...they come up with loads of reasons to "Justify" forking over their hard earn cash, but that just makes them FEEL better about spending the money. That FEELING they get from thinking about owning, driving, using, and having that product is what we can label, EMOTION.

EMOTION AXIOM: *Emotion trumps need every time.*
SAY THAT OVER 5 TIMES!!
So let's examine emotion under the magnifying glass of NEED. In other words the more closely

someone looks at buying something, the more emotional they may get about it, the more they feel like they "Need" it, when actually they may not have a major need for it. In truth, they WANT it, and EMOTION created that WANT over need.

Examples are, the **SMELL** of the new car when they test drive it, the **FEEL** of the leather seats, the **SOUND** of the powerful engine they don't actually NEED, as opposed to a smaller less powerful engine, that would fulfill their actual need. It's the **LOOK** of the sleek lines of the aerodynamic sportier model, rather than the boxy lines of the family sedan, which does one thing, it creates EMOTION!
Finally they think, "What the heck, we've only got two kids they can sit in the half seat in the back."
EMOTION TRUMPS NEED EVERY TIME!

In the last paragraph the bolded words illustrate how some of the things that can create this emotion in a potential buyer. The first rule for new car salespeople is, "Get them in the car", then they CAN experience all the things mentioned, but what if you're not selling new cars? How can you stir up emotion about other not so emotional products?

In every product there's got to be something that you can make "Sizzle". If nothing else it's the money they will MAKE with it or by using it, or the money they will SAVE, or how it will make their life easier. How you "Paint the picture", is how you make them FEEL about the your product or service. If you paint a blurred or sketchy picture because you don't know all the details which would make that "Picture" emotional, you most likely will get a blurred and sketchy answer when you say, "Can we write it up for you now?" Probably something like, "Well I'll have to check with xxxx and we'll have to think about it."

Since the dawn of time people have been fighting between their wants and their needs, and unless it boils down to actual survival, WANTS usually win out. It's a very non-typical happening when someone's needs and wants happen to be aligned to even be on the "Same page" of their life's plan. We all come to the place several times a day when we realize we NEED something, and most of the time it's something that is going to help us do a job, complete an action or some other "Non-emotional" task for us, but at the same time an important task or very important job.

Most of the time the task is not related to enjoyment, fun, or something that we just can't wait to do. But, if we CAN make it something that is FUN, or enjoyable then now we have a whole new category to put it in and we can actually turn it into a WANT.

A good example would be, driving to work. We are going some place that we NEED to go, not necessary someplace we WANT to go, unless of course you work at the Playboy Mansion, or the local ski resort as an instructor.

We get into our car, and we've driven the route many times before, so it's no major happening, and it's an automatic thing without a lot of emotion.

Now let's change that situation a little. A friend is out of town and he/she says you can use their knocked out, souped up sports car to drive every day until they get back.

You can't wait to get up a little early, to GO TO WORK! You want to make sure you have all your things together for work, so you can leave a little earlier. You want to get a parking spot right in front of the main entrance so everyone can see you pull in with this amazing ride. Maybe even sit there a while and listen to the great new stereo system playing your favorite tunes.

What just happened? Your NEED (driving to work) has just become your WANT.

Your job as a master closer salesperson, is to make your client/customer's NEEDS their WANTS. One of the best ways to do this is to sell the SIZZLE instead of the steak, and the way you sell sizzle is with excitement and energy. The attitude YOU have with the client/customer is infectious. Meaning, YOUR level of energy is transferred to THEIR persona. If YOU have energy all around you, and are excited about your product or service, THEY are going feel the same way.

So, if when you get up in the morning, and you feel like you want to stay in bed...DO IT.

A sales floor or environment is no place for a

weak limp wristed attitude and a person with a low energy level. You need to hit the floor in the morning like lightning on a stick, and everyone around you will pick up on this, and pretty soon you've got the joint jump'in!

One of the best ways of starting the day with a positive and energized attitude is to jump out of bed, and immediately slap both hands together and say, "Today is going to be a GREAT day!" This uses two things to reprogram you inner mind.

1. Audio: You hear yourself giving yourself an audio command that it's going to be a great day. This goes into your subconscious mind, (which is the controller of all your behavior) and sets the level and tone of your daily expectations.

2. Physical: Slapping your hands together brings a physical feeling into the situation, and adds to the level of programming you just imparted. This physical input is a very powerful reprogrammer of your subconscious mind and once programmed it is like a heat seeking missile that never misses it's target.

It's not so much as what YOU do, it's what your inner mind TELLS you to do, and unless it's programmed to tell you the right things, you are not going to DO the right things. Unless you know where you're going, how do you know when you get there.
So, you've got positive audio and physical input to start your day, along with a goal that you WILL realize. "It's going to be a great day."

Now just go and sell the SIZZLE!

Your energy and enthusiasm will be a contiguous force that others will pick up all around you. Don't ask or wonder if it's going to help or if it's going to work...
JUST DO IT!

CHAPTER 22
LEARNING TO CHANGE

You may think, "Change, what change, I don't need to change, I'm fine just the way I am".

If you were doing everything perfect you wouldn't be trying to figure ways to be a better sales person, make more money, and remember, that's why you're reading this book!

That's the thinking of 80% of the salespeople right now, in jobs where they feel like they should be closing more deals. However; they say, "The economy is bad, the leads are old and used up, people have no money" and the list of "Can't do it", goes on.

Everyone has a perception of themselves, and it's how they THINK they are perceived by other people, and intern perceived by themselves. This perception of themselves and their abilities is what gets them where they are right now.

Look around you. If you don't like where you are in life now, first realize that you can change it. First of all you must realize that everything that happens to you, everyone you have attracted TO you, and everything you have at this moment, is BECAUSE of YOU.

If you don't like it, change it. The problem with change is, it takes WORK, and you have to WANT to do it. It's not something that you can put in the oven like a loaf of bread dough, and in 15 minutes it comes out ready for toast and butter.

Change is a "Hands on" type of effort, and we are talking about YOUR hands here.

Another problem with change is, there is an "Old Man or Old Woman" inside us that violently resists change, because change is uncomfortable, and takes a lot of work. It also may give us a lot of new challenges and hurdles to jump over, and everyone knows how difficult that is.

Here is a scenario that illustrates the process of change with in us. It's from my first book, "Winning, it's a lot more FUN!"

THE OLD MAN

How many of us like change? You work hard to achieve your station in life, to get things going your way, and you seem to have gotten a handle on all of it...you think. Then along comes a new idea, a concept, or a different way of thinking and doing. It looks real and is a totally different method of getting to what you think is a higher level of achievement than you have ever reached. We're not only talking about sports here, we could be talking about area of your life or skill that you would like to improve upon. In order to climb to a higher level they say you have to change this or that about what you are now doing, and you may have to start over in parts of what you want to improve. Suddenly it all starts to take on a whole new and sometimes "Ugly" picture of what you thought you were just trying to make better.

Take the story about the woodsman. He's chopping down trees to build his log cabin, and somebody walks by as says, "You know, if you got a chainsaw you could cut down a lot more trees, and a lot quicker too". So he goes to town and buys a chainsaw, comes back and gets a quarter of the way through a tree and it quits. Goes back to the hardware store asks what's wrong. The store owner says, "You needed to mix the oil with the gas to get it to work properly". He does this, goes back to the woods, cuts half way through the tree, saw quits cutting...back to the store again. Owner says, "You gotta learn something about chainsaws here pardoner, it needs sharpening. You see if you expect it to keep cutting, you gott'a buy a file sharpener." He buys the file, gets back to the woods, discovers it's the wrong size of file sharpener for that particular saw...back to the store, and gets the right file. Now he's ready to do some major cutting. He cuts almost all the way through the tree and runs out of gas. Well, it was dark by then anyway. Next morning you see him swinging his axe!

Does this sound like a situation you may have been a part of at one time in your life? You see a new idea, concept or way to improve your sales closure ratio, customer service, marketing effort, or anything in your life. You try it, and before long you find yourself on a flaming skateboard flying down hill in to a lake of gasoline...or so it seems.

That's the way it is when you are trying effect mental control, and belief system change, to give you outward, and recognizable change, in dollars and cents. Which, by the way is a good method of how you keep score in the sales business. More money does not *always* mean you are a successful salesperson, but it IS a good way of identifying more people buying from you, and more people RE-buying from you. This, is a clear indication that you are doing a few things correctly and an indicator of a successful sales campaign or salesperson.

The skills necessary to develop successful customer interaction, product presentation, and closing techniques, can be learned through reading, and sales training. The big problem is, teaching someone to actually CARE about the customer, and have a focused intent on their satisfaction, in getting what best fits their needs while in keeping with their wants.

You have a belief system, and this belief system is responsible for you *allowing* yourself to be successful, because you truly believe you are a winner, or in this case close more business...or finding a way to lose that supports the idea that you "Tried really hard anyway!"

One of the purposes of this book is to help you change this belief system, and actually SEE yourself being successful with all types of personalities, and customers.

DO YOU NEED TO CHANGE?

Ask yourself, "Are you a person who is always searching for a "Better way". Are you one of the modern day explorers of our time? The master closer, or truly powerful salesperson, is always looking for new methods of improving their skills, and their craft. Although they may not really NEED to change much about themselves, they WANT to change for the sake of betterment, and to constantly be improving themselves.

CHANGE is what keeps energy in our lives, prevents stagnation, and provides challenge.

You are most likely one of these people, or you wouldn't be reading this book in the first place!

Unless you are a person who INVITES change, enjoys diversity, and welcomes a challenge you need to take a close look at that thing we call "Self-image".

CHANGE in what you believe you can accomplish, what you THINK you deserve and how you go about things in your life, is something that most people not only will walk away from, but also run away from. They like the status quo, and have grown "Comfortable", with the way things are. "THINGS", however; never say the same, and are always changing regardless of what we do or how we believe.

If YOU are the person who initiates the changes for the positive, and betterment, then YOU are in the control position, not "Things", and things left to themselves very rarely improve on their own.

Mechanical parts get rusty if not used, and your

body gets weak, and stiff if not stressed and exercised? The saying, "Use it or lose it", can be applied to almost any area of our lives, and sales is no exception.

Some people probably feel they could just skip over this chapter and say, "I'm doing ok here, there's nothing wrong with what I'm doing", and they could be right.

But, very few, and again I say VERY few could in all correctness, can ever get away with saying or even thinking that.

So it is for these greater masses of salespeople that are very good at what they do, and also for the knowledge seeking beginners, that I say, "Good job at self-evaluation, and welcome upper level thinking, over-achievers in our society."

This is what the master closers do, this is their skill set. They SEE themselves closing each and every customer that comes into their sphere of influence. This may not happen all the time but their belief system bears up statistics that support this, they act like a winner, think like a winner and they ARE a winner at the end of the day, and the end of the month.

It depends how much passion you have towards the image of being successful. How much dedication will you give to an effort that WILL make you a better salesperson. ARE you willing to change certain things about your personality and character, in order to come up to a higher standard of successful selling?

MATERIALIZATION AXIOM: When you see it happen in your mind, it soon becomes reality, how soon it happens depends how real and clear you saw it.

RESISTANCE

It seems the older people get the more they resist change, hence the saying, "You can't teach an old dog new tricks". There is an "Old man" in all of us that resists change. This "Old Man" sometimes will resist violently keeping us from making the changes necessary to climb to a higher level of proficiency or attain a higher rung on the ladder of life. This is in anything we do and being the best salesperson in your company, or just increasing your sales is only one of them.

Change in our belief system is the most difficult change to make on a deeper level within us. This "Old man" we're talking about, will resist violently because he (or she) likes the comfort of what's already established, likes the known set of problems to be dealt with, and doesn't want any more NEW problems. This Old Man can actually cause you to do worse in order to get you to "Go back" to what you used to do, or what you used to think, in order to preserve the status quo. Then when you actually do worse, you will say, "Yeah, I better stick with what I know", and this Old Man can go back to being comfortable in his little world of mediocrity and being anything but number one.

Think of it this illustration. In order to climb higher, sometimes you have to get on a "Taller ladder" and you don't just "Jump" from one ladder to the other. This means you have to climb DOWN to get off the ladder you are on, so you can start climbing UP the new ladder to a higher level. Also, maybe that "New ladder" is more difficult to climb because the "Rungs" are farther apart, very slippery, and it's slow going, but you don't let it stop you. You can see how far up the ladder goes, and you know you are going to reach the top.

If there is something you feel you need to change about your sales approach, product knowledge, or your methods, first research it thoroughly, or ask a credible source for advice. When it comes to mental change, approach it with an open mind. Remember, it's the Old Man who will always keep you from new learning, new concepts, and the quest for expanding your thinking.

Oliver Wendell Holmes once said, *"The mind, once expanded to the dimensions of larger ideas, never returns to its original size."*

When you set out on the quest to change your belief system to make you a consistent winner, in any phase of your life, you set in motion a very powerful goal seeking mechanism.

Our brain was meant to serve us like a very powerful computer; it will literally do what we tell it. The trick is, HOW we tell it to do our bidding, makes all the difference in the world. We program it each and every day with what we say when we talk to ourselves, this programming is then stored in our mental warehouse of information. The Old Man is the guard at the door of this warehouse and the more comfortable he becomes by not having to put new information, and concepts into it, the better he likes it. So you decide to start reprogramming this powerful computer of yours called the Subconscious Mind, by the use of mental reprogramming Cds and DVDs or self-improvement books. You decide to restructure your ideas about yourself as a winner, along with the visualizations of winning, it is in direct conflict with what this Old Man wants...CHANGE!

He will fight you all of the way, and may even make you take a step backwards to make you THINK what you're doing will not, or is not working. You need to keep listening to your chosen reprogramming source, or CD. DO NOT give up, sometimes people tell me that they go for several weeks and nothing is happening, things even got worse. Then in one 24 hour period, it all came together like finally breaking through the ice you've been trying to chop through on a frozen lake. It was like a bolt of lightning, the change was so overpowering. It was like all the work, training, and perseverance came together at once, and a great block was removed, they climbed to the top of the mountain...and they never looked back.

In your quest to have this breakthrough, remember to fight the Old Man, don't let him win, you have to keep hammering away at him, keep the pressure on. If you start to do worse because of changes you made, if you start to get irritable, it's usually a sign that the Old Man is about to give in. He's giving it one more try to make you give up and go back to being comfortable with the old state of being. It's a sign that you are very close to a break through in your quest for change, and effort to excel to a higher level. If it was easy, we'd all be playing our favorite sport on T.V., live in the house on the hill, drive the Bentley, and more. So...hang in there, fight the Old Man, and get ready to jump into the winner's circle, because your breakthrough is just around the corner.

JUST DO IT

CHAPTER 23
A SOLUTION FOR EVERY OBSTACLE

People can be divided into two groups, those with positive tendencies, and those with negative tendencies.

Positive people see the good, and positive traits in others, and how any situation can be made to end up with a winning, positive solution. These people don't need to have someone micro-managing them to make sure they get to work on time, leave on time, and while they're at work they WORK. They are natural problem solvers, coming up with the solutions to all the "Little things" that end up becoming BIG things if not dealt with properly and timely. These are the people that before long are asked to become "Managers" in their department, and eventually rise to the top of their company.

This attitude can be taught, but not as successfully to people who have been raised in a negatively slanted home or environment.

Negative people are the first ones to comment on why something won't work, doesn't work, and will end up in disaster if left the way it currently is without change. They focus on what might happen that is of a negative nature, or make the plan "Fall through." It's more important for them to distance themselves from a negative situation than to gravitate toward a positive one.

You can "Suggest" to them to be more positive,

command them to look on the positive side, and straight out tell them you can't use them if they cannot BECOME a more positive person, at least while at work. However; causing a predominately negatively biased person to become a more positive one, is usually a losing battle.

If you want to accept that challenge, the best way is to lead by example, and show them "Real time" how LIVING in a positive environment works.

Each group has the same kinds of traits, and behavior, only at opposite ends of the spectrum.

POSITIVE PEOPLE ARE:
SOLUTION based
Find answers to questions
Enjoy a challenge
Welcome change
Do more that expected of them

NEGATIVE PEOPLE ARE:
PROBLEM based
Asking questions without answers
Trying to avoid challenges
Resisting change
Do only what is expected of them

When searching for a solution to a problem that presents itself in any sales situation or objection, you need to come up with it immediately or a.s.a.p.

Therefore you need to clarify these

problems/objections long before they arise in the sales presentation or situation. These solutions must be focused and tackle the real objection as the first reply out of your mouth, and seem like you just thought of it.

THE SOLUTION IN DISGUISE

With every problem or hurdle there IS a solution. That solution might not be apparent at the time, but just knowing that there is a solution out there somewhere, is what drives the master closer on toward a positive answer to that problem.

The solution to the problem or obstacle may be staring you right in the face, or may be embedded IN the problem. It's the master closer or just someone with a positive viewpoint, has the ability to realize it.

EXAMPLE: This really happened at a screening for the Miss Universe pageant. One of the girls was asked as a general knowledge question, "Who wrote **Beethoven's** 9th symphony in D minor". Her response, "Ah, I'm not really into music so I can't even make a guess, but isn't that a little difficult for the first question?" DUH!

The only reason I submit this is to illustrate the instance where the ANSWER is hidden (and not very well) in the question. With each and every problem there always is a solution, it just depends on your degree of positive perception to be able to recognize that solution, and a.s.a.p.

Once you truly believe that there is a positive answer for ANY question, then you start seeing, hearing and realizing more and more answers and solutions to problems. You might even surprise yourself at what you come up with for ways to solve every problem you encounter.

SOLUTION AXIOM: NOTHING IS AS EASY OR AS HARD AS IT LOOKS TO ACCOMPLISH THE *SECOND* TIME YOU LOOK AT IT.

Being able to turn a negative situation into a positive one is the hallmark of a master closer. Some people are just positive type people in general. You don't have to TEACH them how to be positive in their perceptions.

I'm sure you've heard the story of the two little boys in the behavioral experiment. Even though you have, I'll document it again for those who haven't.

Psychologists were trying to understand what made some people positive in nature and the others somewhat less than positive. They figured "Let's take two children and try to learn when positive or negative behavioral patterns start, or are learned.
They took two little boys about 7 years old and put them in two different situations.

One little boy came from a home that was quite affluent and was given almost everything he wanted all the time.

The other one was from a moderate income home and was in opposite contrast to his counterpart.

The little "Rich kid" was put in a room with all the newest toys and fun things to play with.

The other little boy was put in a room full of horse manure.

Pretty soon the boy in the "Fun room" was complaining that there were not enough toys, and they were old toys that have been on the market for weeks, and began to whine, and gripe on how he wanted the newest thing on the market.

The other little boy in the room full of horse manure was grabbing it throwing it the air saying, "With all this horse poop on the floor, it must mean there's a pony in here somewhere."

Once again, it's YOUR ***perception*** of the event at hand, not the actual reality of the event that makes the difference.

Always ask yourself the question, "What is my perception of this event, positive or negative. There is no middle ground, it's either positive or negative. The positive type person says, "I *can* do it, or find out how it can be done. The negative type person says, "If I can't do it I'll spend more time trying to find a way to justify why I failed."

Your belief system is what gets you where you are, gives you what you have, and is responsible for who you become in life. It attracts either great opportunities, good chances, good people, or just the opposite, depending on how positive or negative you see things.

There is nobody else, no outside factors, YOU are the magnet that attracts TO you what you now have and who you have become or WILL become.

The U.S. Marines have a saying that I love to quote. "For things that are difficult, we do right away, the impossible takes a little longer!"

Which one are you? In sales, the master closers are the ones who never take no AS and answer, never even consider failure as an option, and are the 10% that sells 90% of the sales.

Think like a winner and you WILL be one, JUST DO IT.

CHAPTER 24
LEAD MANAGEMENT

OK, so you work your tail off to get, leads, referrals, phone numbers of friends of friends, and anyone who may want to buy what you're selling. How do you handle it all?

That's a big question, and how you answer it may be the key to your success or the pitfall to your undoing. When you consider the fact that one phone number, one name or one meeting can make the difference in getting a sale, completing a contract or just cementing one relationship, then you realize the importance of proper IM (Information Management).

If you treat each piece of information as if it were a treasured gold coin, then you are starting to put an "Information value" on the data you are bringing in to your sphere of existence. You can't use it until you GET it, then after you get it, what do you do with it?

CRM SOFTWARE

Customer Retention Management, that's what CRM stands for, and although the word is RETENTION, is should also be noted that it could be changed to PROCUREMENT software. Until you talk to them you cannot RETAIN them. There are several CRMs out there, ACT, GOLDMINE, and SALES FORCE, are the three main products, and they all have one thing in common. They transcribe the contact information, what was said on the call, when to call back, level of interest, and incidental information about that particular lead.

When you realize the importance of each one of these leads and the fact that each one is just as important as the other, no matter what the name, or where it came from, then you are beginning to get a handle on lead management.

If you don't have CRM software, you can make a simple CRM chart on a piece of paper. All you want to do is note who they are, their contact info, what they want, when to get back to them, is there another decision maker to talk to, and the level of interest they have in your product or service.

It's always good to get some personal information about them, age, occupation, kids, grandkids, spouse's name, why they inquired and of course WHEN to call them back.

Use a word processing program to create it, or if you don't have a computer do it on a plain sheet of paper and a ruler to make lines, vertical and horizontal to separate the info. It's not rocket science. You just need to know who they are, what they want, how and when to call them back, and some personal info about them. Sometimes it's the personal information that you later mention that shows them you are interested in them as a person and not just a commission/sale.

Ask probing questions as much as possible without making them ask you, "What'aya writing a book or something?" The more info you can get about someone the better you can tailor your presentation to be just what they need to hear, and none of what will waste their time. It's all part of that very important thing called "Getting rapport".

THE PRICE OF INFORMATION

Here is probably the most important consideration on obtaining the information you want to be able to manage. The old saying, "You get what you pay for", is a very true statement in just about anything you want to acquire. Good leads of people that "May" be in the market for what you are selling, needs to be given a high degree of priority.

You've probably heard the statement, "He's so good he could sell snow to an Eskimo". It's an old simile that illustrates someone's ability to sell something to someone who's already GOT too much of what's for sale.

It doesn't matter how "Good" of a salesperson you are, there is absolutely no way you are going to be able to sell your product or service to people who either, have got more of it that you have, don't have a need for it , and don't have the money anyway if they DID want it.

Now it comes down to not only being good at what you do in sales, but also having the "Right" customers/clients to talk to, who have a justifiable need for your product or service you are selling.

So in this case, we are talking about the price of the LEADS. Where to do you get them, and how do you manage them when you do get them.

There are lead brokers by the dozens out there who are trying to sell YOU something, LEADS. These leads have different levels of credibility and this level of credibility has a price. The newer the lead the higher the price, and the more pre-qualified the lead. With that in mind, you have a greater chance to connect with someone who will not hang up on you, eventually end up in a sale. This will hopefully end up in a commission for you. Which, again is the reason you're reading this book!

Knowing this, let's look at some criteria for evaluating leads and see why they cost what they do.

CURRENT INFORMATION

This should probably be considered at the top of the list in importance when considering actually PAYING for leads. If the name of the person you call gets you a response like, "He died last year", it does not matter how little you paid for that lead, it was TOO MUCH!

Each lead you buy will either produce one of 5 things.

1. Someone who wants what you're selling and a possible new client/customer.
2. Someone who MAY want what you're selling.
3. Someone who has no idea of what you're selling, and just needs someone to talk to and will waste your time.
4. Someone who will tell you they are on the DON'T CALL list and to never call you again.
5. Someone who is not even the person for which you are calling, doesn't even know them, and has never known them.

Once a lead gets to be over 6 months old, you can pretty well figure it to be on the bottom rung of the information ladder. That's not to say all 6 month old leads are worthless, but in that time people move, die, already buy what you're selling, and become what we call "Time wasters".

It's very wise when purchasing leads to ask if they have a refund policy for wrong numbers, deceased people, move-outs, and disconnects.

If so, there is a better chance of the leads you do actually receive being more credible, or at least not being disconnected.

WARM LEADS
These are people that have responded to some kind of advertising that you, or the company you work for has put in place. They responded because they were actually looking for what you're selling. Sometime it is because they were on the company's web site, or got a mailer, saw an advertisement, or in some way already know

something about the product or service you represent. These people are GOLD, treat them as gold, in that you keep very precise records of when they were called, did you leave a message on their voice mail, did you talk to them directly, what was the result, and when to call them back.

PRE-SCREENED LEADS

Now here is where it begins to get expensive, but most of the time well worth it. First of all let us discuss the level of "Pre-screening".

Number Verification

The lowest level of pre-screening is phone number verification. That means simply, "Does the phone number work or not". If you or your sales force is dialing the phone all day, and half of the numbers are disconnected, then you have a lot of wasted time invested. When you begin to pay more for leads it's with an understanding that the numbers are genuine and are still in working order, and you usually get a refund for disconnected numbers.

Customer name verification

This means someone actually TALKS to the person on the other end to verify that they are the person with the name on the lead. Now we are getting a little more expensive, and as you may have guessed, the more "Funneled down" the lead is, the more expensive it is.

So, consider the value of the time you or your sales force spends, in dialing phone numbers, asking for specific people by name, only to find that they don't live here any more, have died, or that they're actually 12 years old! It may well be a very worthwhile practice to pay more for pre-screened leads in this situation.

Exclusivity

This means how many times were these leads sold to other competitors of yours, and in turn how many times they have ALREDY been called. The more exclusive the lead, the more expensive it is going to cost.

Customer interest verification

Now we are talking about some money to be spent here. This is where the "Qualifier" asks the person on the lead if they would have an interest in what is being sold or offered, and if they would like to receive a call back from one of the agents to discuss the product or service.

This type of lead is truly worth whatever you pay for it, because it is information that most likely will result in a sale, by even a beginner salesperson, and a sale is a sale.

In any case, you have to evaluate how much each sale will bring in relation to how much you pay for that lead. When a company is going to close a client who will pay $2,000 to $3,000 for their service, then $25 a lead for someone who is interested, motivated and wants a call back, is a good bargain.

CHAPTER 25
SCRIPT WRITING

Every good sales organization or phone room has got to have a "Script" to start off their new salespeople, and especially to keep the existing salespeople on track. There is just absolutely no way you can be able to start pitching a product or service "Off the cuff" or spontaneously. This would be considered "Make it up as you go along, and that is not good, not even acceptable. If you've ever listened to someone who doesn't really know the product or service, you hear a spewing of filler words or sounds like "Ah, er, well ah, uhm, I ah. Pretty soon there's more filler words or phrases than there are words or phrases that have meaning or content, and the client/customer is thinking, "Is this person ever going to get to the point?"

The second thing this kind of behavior does is make people think that you don't know or have any idea of what you're talking about, and that blows away any level of confidence the customer/client may have about you in the first interaction. Once that confidence level is challenged it's almost impossible to get it back, so you may as well just hang up and dial another number AFTER you DO know what you're talking about.

Writing a winning script that will actually result in sales, it a very challenging assignment. You have to condense down what the product or service is actually about, and be able to CONVEY it to someone in the short time that you have their

attention on the phone after they say "Hello". Usually to be very effective you need to bring out the main advantage of the product or service, in the first 30 seconds, to "Shock" the customer/client into realizing they are listening to someone who can bring them a major saving, major clients, or do something that is outside the "Envelope" of average. You need to portray the product or service as so much better than what they are now getting from whatever program in which they are participating. This message needs to be conveyed in the fewest amount of words or phrases, so it will gain you an "Audience" with the person with which you are talking. It's got to make them LISTEN to you, because they instantly sense the possible benefit they will get by saying "Yes" to you in the end.
There are 4 areas of the pitch that need to be considered to develop a good script.

CONTENT – TONE – TEMPO – COMMANDS

Content simply means the MEANING of the words you are using. When someone writes a script they need to pack as much meaning into as few words as possible. When you do this you need to avoid words that covey mediocrity, average, usual, and casual references. Specifically they would be words like "Possibly, usually, may work, better that average, in line with, good, ok, and anything else that does not depict the "Best, most powerful, and totally best" reference.

LINGUISTICS: The meaning of language/words

Another thing to keep in mind is, that all words do not mean the same thing to all people. In the discipline of NLP that we talked about earlier, LINGUISTICS is the study of what words actually mean for different people. Each person you will be delivering this pitch to has a set of different belief systems, feelings, and definitions for just about every word or phrase you are going to include in this script. Keep in mind that when you use a phrase or group of words that may mean a certain thing or convey a certain feeling to YOU it might not have the same effect to the person on the other end of the phone. This is either consciously or **sub**consciously. This is *especially* true if you are talking to a person of foreign birth or nationality.

CONTRACTIONS: For instance, if you're writing a script that will be directed primarily to foreigners, DO NOT use contractions. They do not understand the words DON'T CAN'T WON'T HASEN'T MUSN'T, and the like. You will be blowing right by them in your explanations and references, and when you get to the end they'll probably say, "We not ***interesting*** right now." Not because they don't want what you have, but because they got LOST along the way and have absolutely know idea of what you just said or even mean.

COLLOQUIALISMS: These are words or phrases that we use as slang, and usually never in written form. Such as "Easy as pie, old as the hills, raining cats and dogs". Avoid these kinds of references because there are some people (again foreigners) who may think you're crazy. They're thinking, *"How could cats and dogs come from sky?"*

Sometimes foreigners try to use these references and they don't get them exactly right or choose the wrong word in the phrase and it's really laughable. Like the guy who tries to rob a bank, goes in and points the gun at the teller and says, "Ok Buddie, this is SITCK-IN, I want all your money and I want it in LARGE WILLIAMS. So much for my stand-up act, but you get the point.

COMMON PHRASES: Some of the common phrases that we all use can have a vast different perception by many people depending upon their background, personal history and subconscious implantation of memories and experiences. For example, when you say something like, "If I can just get a method of payment today, we can *BRING YOU ON BOARD* right away." That's a nice way of asking for the payment, but what if the person you're talking to hates boats, gets sea sick, and almost drowned in an boating accident? Coming "On board" may activate a subconscious response in this person that is very

uncomfortable, and even make them queasy, let alone NOT want to continue talking with you!
So, carefully analyze each word in your script to determine if you have any double meaning possibilities, references to things that may be connected to memories or experiences that could be in any way negative with your client/customer.

AUTHENTICATORS
These are words or phrases that tell someone that just BECAUSE you know the term or phrase, you are very knowledgeable about the subject, product or specific area in which you are making reference. For instance if you were talking to a real estate client and you mentioned the fact that their attorney had a "Fiduciary" responsibility to them in looking over their contract etc....that would say a lot about your knowledge of law, attorneys, and the legal system.
So, you know the jargon of your product or service, makes sure you sprinkle a few authenticators into your pitch, and conversation with your new clients/customers. Much can be said "Between the lines" as we all know, so never forget the words you use and choose them wisely. It could make the difference between sale and no sale.

NEGATIVE/POSITIVE SOUNDS
Did you realize that linguistics experts have come up with words and sounds that they claim are

more pleasing than other words and phrases that they claim are less pleasing and even irritating. Below are a list of the irritating words they suggest NOT to use in a sales presentation. They are called the H sound words.

Hunger, hornets, hussy, hard, hit, horrible, hot, hellish, hell, hardcore, hit, hateful. These are just words that have a "Hard" sound to them. Avoid them in a sales presentation or sales script if you can.

GOOD WORDS OR SOUNDS

Now for the better, more soothing sounding words that tend to put people at ease, and in a comfortable state. These are words that evoke positive reactions, and states.

Winning, wise, wants, worship, willing, welcome wealth, well, well being, wonderful, and willful.

"V" words are also great because they have the same effect on people. Some examples are:

Venus, valet, very, varsity, victory, Vanguard, velvet, and very good.

These are just examples of how you can structure your presentation or pitch to be more pleasing to your client/customer. In then end if it works JUST DO IT, but don't discount it without trying/using it.

CHAPTER 26
THE FEAR OF SUCCESS

You're probably asking yourself right now, "Did I just read that title right?" Yes it said fear of winning. By now your thought of running to the copy machine to bump off a few copies of this chapter has just quickly subsided, and you're wondering if you tear it out of the book, you can hit the wastebasket with it from where you're sitting?

But, before you do, here is an EXCERSISE: go back to the time when it looked like there was no possible WAY you could lose in one kind of a competition or another. A sales situation, a board meeting, a time where the sale was a guaranteed "Laydown".

Here we're not talking only sales, but all, and any of the competitions that stand out in your life. These could be on the field of competitive sports battles, pool hall, the boardroom, the living room, the locker room, or anywhere when your quickness of thought, muscle, action or reaction was required. In this competition you were a sure thing...but something happened, you LOST, or things didn't go your way!
There was no possible way (in your mind) that you could lose or come close to losing in the situation confronting you. Still when the final points were tallied, the votes were in, the score

was added up, the contract was signed (or not signed)...it didn't end the way you planned.

If that sounds like you at some point in your life, don't throw this article away just yet!

You MAY have been the victim of being afraid to win. Yes, the fear of winning is a true reality for all of us who haven't established our crown of prowess and achievement. It is always lurking in the face of pressure, and in the minds of the established champions, the master closers, the top sales managers, and corporate heads, just as much as the "Newbie".

OK, now that you know about the fear of winning, you probably are wondering just how this can happen?

Let's examine some of the reasons why you can be afraid of winning or closing that big deal.

REASON #1
I DON'T DESERVE IT.

Maybe you had a fight with your spouse, or your boss or your co-worker, or your child, or whoever, and you said some things that were completely out of character for you. Now you feel you have damaged someone, and because you *PRECIEVE* yourself in reality, as a good caring person, this sets up a conflict with your self-image that turns you upside down. "If I'm so good why did I have such a conflict with that person that I value as an important part of my life?"

Maybe it's because I'm NOT as good as I think,

and I DON'T deserve to win, maybe I'm NOT as good as I imagine myself".
This could go on and on, and so you miss too many closing opportunities, the customer senses indecision in you, lack of confidence, and the sale slips away and...you LOSE!

Sound familiar? It's just the tip of the iceberg on the fear of winning, brought on by the incorrect perception that you DO NOT DESERVE TO WIN.

REASON # 2
HOW IT WILL CHANGE MY LIFE.
You may think deep down, "If I close this next deal, get this next sale, if I'm successful THIS time, I'm home free, I'll win the sales contest, get the corner office, the big desk, that promotion I THINK I deserve."

BUT...what if I do, I'll be a WINNER... and then my life will be upside down with pressure on me to keep winning. I'll have to work harder to stay in the winner's circle, people will be looking to me for advice, what if I don't keep winning, they will look down on me. It will be worse that if I just stay in my comfortable little lovable loser spot and keep plodding along at my own pace. I like it here in my comfortable number 2, 3 or 4 spot, I'm afraid to be a winner because I'd have to say goodbye to this comfort level, and I don't want to do that."

REASON #3
I DON'T KNOW HOW TO ACT
"What will I do if I win?", you may think. "I've

never won before so I might not know what to say, I might say something stupid, and I might come off as a dummy. I hate being in the limelight."

You conjure up all these ideas of how you're not that level of "Winner", you're not comfortable around people "Of that level". Once again it comes down to a LEVEL...OF...COMFORT! You want the money, but are not comfortable with that "Level of success"! You have a FEAR OF SUCCESS, because it challenges your BELIEF SYSTEM!

What you *believe*, you can *achieve*.

You've got to embrace your fears, wrap your arms around those fears, rub up against them, get in close to that thing that makes you scream. You'll find out it doesn't have as many teeth as you imagined and may just become your friend. Embrace all those "People" who you thought were "Too good for you, in another league, above your station in life", and you will find that they're really not that much different.

So many times, it's not the people, it's not the event, and it's not the situation that you think is beyond your grasp, it's your VIEW of the event, the people, or the situation you are facing.

The FEAR AXIOM:
Fear is only the PROJECTION of an unrealized negative POSSIBILITY that may, or may not, ever become real.

Now let's not get KAA RAZZIE...sometimes fear is a good thing that helps us preserve our existence, whether it's in the pool room or the board room, but it must be tempered with a solid dose of reality. In sales, having the ability to present variables, and advantages of our product or service to our potential client/customers, is a very important skill. But it's a little like the guy betting $100 he could walk across a 12 inch wide plank for 50 feet. He had all the confidence in the world until he was told it was going to be between two buildings, 100 feet in the air. Pressure is what breaks our concentration and shakes our confidence.

The more that's at stake, the more we doubt our skills and ability to make the right choice, or come through with the "Goods". It's still the same plank, just more to lose if we falter, so it has a negative effect of every part of our mind and body.

If we feel we don't deserve it, we don't belong, or we are not as good as our competition, that "Plank" looks smaller and higher than it really is. Once again, it's more of our VIEW of how we THINK things are than how they really are.

It's that VIEW of our work, our ability, and our power to make good things happen for us, that can attract the best or the worst life has to offer.

CHANGING YOUR VIEW

So how you change your view of the situation,

challenge at hand, or up coming confrontation or battle?

Take stock of all your assets, you know your limits, and you've probably come close to the edge of those limits, and still ended up a winner many times.

Re-live those times, mentally re-examine those triumphs, and victories. SEE and FEEL the sweet taste of winning and victory, and apply that same winning attitude to your new up-coming challenges.

You WILL be the winner, or at least walk away thinking "I did what I felt was my best, and THAT makes me a winner no matter what"!

Change your VIEW and you change your reality, along with changing the end result of what you THOUGHT you could accomplish.

PRACTICE

Spend a small amount of time actually sitting in a comfortable chair or couch and just RELAX. Let your mind go loose and limp, like a wet dish rag. Then go back to a time of victory and winning for you, in your mind, and relive that winning situation all over again. See, hear, smell and feel, all the sensations and events of that experience. Get the same feeling you got when it you triumphed.

Now carry that feeling and power into your next challenge, and you WILL be a winner, because

you already FEEL like a winner.
JUST DO IT!

REASON # 3
OTHERS WILL BE JEALOUS OF ME
I'll make people mad at me. All the people who I surpass will be jealous of me and won't like me anymore.

Is it that important to you to be liked by people who would probably "Throw you under the bus", in a heartbeat if it meant they would be "Top salesperson", get the corner office, and the private secretary etc., if they outdid you?

Never forget the first rule of SALES!

SELL SELL SELL

Your first purpose and dedication is to... (ready for this)... SELL!

Never compare yourself to anyone else, and you will never have a "Skewed view of reality". You will never feel better or worse than your fellow salespeople, and you will always maintain a good grasp of how things are developing around you.

When you are good at what you do, handle client/customers with respect, and skill, you will become a top salesperson as a by-product of these skills. So, actually what you WANT to do is MAKE other salespeople jealous of you, by being credible, and honest with all of your client/customers. This will have them coming back, referring their friends to you, and THAT'S why you are considered "Top Salesperson".

REASON # 4
I'LL HAVE TO WORK HARDER

In order to keep wining I'll have to learn more, build my knowledge of the products/services, work harder and put more time in the office or workplace, just to stay up with the other top people who are winners on a regular basis. I like it where I am, and don't want to put more time in than I am now doing.

The great tennis star Jimmy Connors was once asked, to what he attributed his long winning streak. He replied, "I guess I just hate losing more that I like winning". What ever it takes for you to develop that winning or "Hate to lose" attitude when you find it, don't forget to USE it. Think of ALLOWING yourself to win rather than driving yourself to keep from losing. You have all the necessary skills now, just get out of your own way, relax and ENJOY the game, keep your eyes on the client or customer and not the pay check.

The pay check should be a "By-product" of your in depth knowledge, your attunement to customer needs, and your ability to achieve rapport with your client/customer.

Some salespeople concentrate more on the paycheck, or the "goal line" than they do their customer needs or wants. When this happens the customer can always tell where the focus lies, and

there goes your pay check that your were so tightly focused on.
Don't WORK at it, just let it happen with honesty, and integrity, customers can tell you have their well being at heart, and they will be back again and again... Just DO IT!

THE SUCCESS CONUNDRUM

What is a conundrum? It is a very puzzling question, situation or event. Sometimes it is a situation that by its very existence contains a factor that is self-defeating or has a destructive action to bring about its own end.

In sales there are quite a few conundrums, and it would be very beneficial to realize this when choosing a field of sales in which to make your mark.

EXAMPLE: The debt settlement business is a field that has what I would call the "No money" conundrum. You are making cold calls or warm calls on people who have a large credit card balance and many times have missed payments and very poor credit rating. In your call you tell them that you can help their situation of bad credit, and large balances owed, by negotiating with their credit card companies, and bring about a lesser balance to be repaid. This is all good and fine, and they act very positive about having you represent them to their creditors, UNTIL you get to the part about how you need a down payment of say, 25% of what they owe to get them started on the "Road to financial freedom". Most of the

time this amount is about $4000 to $6000, and they tell you, "If I had that kind of money I wouldn't need your help in the first place."
You tell them they could put it on their credit card, and they ask you, "You mean the one that's all maxed out?"

So herein lies the conundrum, you are talking to people who don't have any money, bad credit, and you are asking them to pay you a fee to reduce their debts and improve their credit, which if it were good enough they wouldn't need you in the first place.

Another kind of situational conundrum in the leasing business works like this. A company leases a certain types of equipment, an example would be for instance, copy machines. These are not new but refurbished copy machines so the print shop owner can save a lot of money in a monthly payment by doing business with a company that presents these types of up to date refurbished machines. This company however uses a 3rd party leasing company much like an auto dealership. You call up print and copy shops and ask them if they are in need of a great refurbished copy machine that will save them a ton of money, and how you provide a lot of other services that will also save them another ton of money. Most of them say they own their own machine, or are on contract to another manufacturer, and a host of other "I not need now" reasons. Then after about 30 or 40 calls, you get one that is VERY responsive, and says they would like to lease one of your machines,

and how fast can they get it?
You have them fill out the leasing forms and later you find out they have been denied for a lease so many times, that their bank wants to repossess YOUR equipment! Just joking, but you get the point.

If they HAD the money they would own their equipment, or already be on a lease with a major bank/lender, and wouldn't need you.

The conundrum is, by the fact that they are so interested, tells you they can't get financing anywhere else and of course they want to talk to you. They think you are a financial wizard, and can do what nobody else could do, get them a lease, and in turn a machine.

Now you're looking for that one needle in the haystack, that has acceptable credit, needs a machine, likes the ones you have to lease, and will give you a try.

If you like rejection, mistreatment, disappointment, and being lied to, THIS is the job for you!

But, then again THAT'S WHAT SALES IS ALL ABOUT!

CHAPTER 27
MANAGEMENT
TO BE OR NOT TO BE

In looking at why you are in sales, you have to ask yourself several questions, and then come up with the most honest answers you can muster. In answering these questions we must quote the

SELF-REALIZATIONS AXIOM: Any question you can ask yourself ABOUT yourself, can be answered BY yourself.

You just have to recognize it as TRUTH when you see it.

This type of thinking represents a big problem with most people. That's why there are so many "Shirnks" or psychotherapists making so much money trying to "Straighten" people out with this same problem of not admitting these levels of truth, and why they have so many problems in life.

But...back to the business of being a manager or laying back and letting someone else shoulder the responsibility. They not only managing the sales activity, writing the sales presentations and scripts, but also keeping track of the employee hours and problems. They have to deal with disgruntled clients, reporting to the owners and stockholders the state of the company and why they are, or are not showing enough profit.

were hired.
It is up to the manager to present these violations in a manner that is not personal, and delivered in a manner that would be consider as firm but as compassionate as possible.

With this kind of interaction with the employee in question, it will ensure the minimal amount of negative results for all concerned.

You should be aware of potential problems that could arise if the person first of all is male, of considerable size or volatile personality. This could become a serious problem. You should alert your security department as to a potential problem so that they are prepared and their response time is cut to a minimum, or just have them on hand at the time.

Company property:
Making certain that the terminated employee takes only their personal items that they brought with them is of paramount importance. This is where you or a security office should be in the room when they are packing up their items.

Sensitive data
If the employee has had access to sensitive company data, special care should be given to monitoring the computer storage items he/she is taking with them, such as flash drives, CDs, and other data storage equipment.

Company access
Any passwords, email programs or all other

company computer data as well as door entry keys, security codes and access data should be changed or eliminated, **BEFORE** the employee is notified of their impending termination.

It will do you no good to have your hard drive erased by this person who feels they should retaliate for being fired. They may delete or erase very important files or data containing contacts and information that were deals and potential deals that could have made you money, along with causing you and the company thousands of dollars in lost information.

You have no "Time machine" there is no rewind, no replay.

I tell people this time and time again, and still when it all "Hits the fan" they say the same thing. "I should 'a taken more care, I should 'a listened better, I should 'a, I should'a, I should'a xxx.

If you think you should'a

JUST DO IT!

CHAPTER 28
BUSINESS VS. PERSONAL LIFE

No matter how you look at it, your business and personal life go hand in hand. In fact if you take a close look at your entire picture of your existence, you can't help but notice the parallels of achievement or under-achievement.

You do great things at your work; good things in your personal life seem to drop in your lap.

Someone said, "The best time to MAKE a sale, is just after you've MADE a sale." This is a concept that is easy to realize, because of the positive energy flow that happens when you accomplish any goal that you've set for yourself.

So, in relation to the two aspects of your life as it relates to your sales position in conjunction with you personal life, the two are more connected that you realize.

Above all that, let's talk about the perspective that controls more of the success, and goal accomplishment in our every day existence, our success in sales, and our success in general at just attaining those "Little victories".

That perspective is what we will call "Your belief system". This is what you truly believe about something, not what your conscious mind tells you what to believe, because you want to get

better at something, or you want to win over an other opponent.
Most people don't even know what their belief system is telling them, or what is on the mental page, unless it gets them in trouble, or they keep getting results in their life that they don't want.

For example it's much harder to attract the things in life that you WANT, rather than the things that you DON'T want. Sometimes it's all you can do to keep from looking at the things you don't want, like having your car booted because you don't have the money for the next payment.

So relating it to the art of selling, if you really really have to have a sale to MAKE that car payment, the desperation shows up in your attitude, your needy persona, and your general aura. People pick up on this, and it is a powerful turnoff, making them think that the only reason you're talking to them is to get a commission, and this means (to them) that you would do anything, say anything, and stoop to any low level to get their money.

The instant someone feels that way, you can most accurately say you have "Lost rapport" with them, and that's the quickest way to lose a sale.

I've seen salespeople going through their presentation when they haven't had a sale all day, all week, all month, etc., and you can feel the tension in their attitude as well as their reactions to any negativity from the customer.

They even get into arguments with the client or customer, and you just want to tell them, "Hang up the phone, and take a break". Because nothing they say will help their situation, all because of their attitude, caused by this belief system.

Someone said, "I don't care if you believe you can do something or not, but one thing is sure...YOU'RE RIGHT. Once again, it all comes back to belief, the degree at which you believe it, the power you put behind that belief, and the amount of work you put behind steps to make it so.

The big question is, how do you get the belief part down firmly when you've never accomplished the task, achieved the goal, or hit the bulls eye to begin with the first time?

One of the best ways is practice, and preparation. If you are prepared for any question, variable, or objection, then even though you may have not got your first sale, YET...you WILL be successful. Then once you get the first level of success, or first trophy of achievement, whatever it might be, you now realize that you CAN do it, you can be successful.

This "Success realization" now carries it's self into all other areas of your life, and those areas begin to bring new victories, and accomplishment.

It's been said that a bad day golfing is better than a good day at work. I strongly disagree with this, because a good day at work (for me at least) is much more rewarding than any recreational experience I could have, let alone golfing, because I suck at golf, even though I try to enjoy it.

Let's take the reverse of that "Work vs. personal life" scenario. Say you have a great day in your recreational or personal life, and now you're at work. You have such a positive attitude, because of winning on the tennis court, golf course, or your kid gets an "A" on his/her report card, and comes home without getting thrown in jail. Right now nothing bothers you, nothing is to difficult to accomplish, and you're on fire! Suddenly sales begin to drop in your lap.

So...it's work, vs. personal life, and when you realize the way the two are intertwined and you can also realize the way that those two parts of your life are actually TOTALLY separate, then you begin to attain some degree of control on both of them.

LIFE VS WORK AXIOM: *Life and work are totally separate, just because you excel or fail at one does not guarantee or even suggest the same results will occur at the other.*

IF you remember this, you will hopefully increase your chances at NOT allowing the negativities of one side of the balance scales of life, to out weigh the other.

This has always been the "Thorn in the side" of many people we could mention, especially the world of sports. Take for example a great golfer or basketball player is involved in sexual misconduct, his endorsements (and a lot of money) go down the drain, he has to spend a lot of money to get OUT of the trouble he has he alone has gotten himself into.

Once again, in this case, it's work vs. personal life, and personal life seems to have a greater effect on work that the other way around.

When your workday is over, you can come home relax, unwind, and most of the time leave the problems behind until the next day whenever you get there.

Obviously this is not a blanket statement, and not all work situations are the same, how your work and personal life relate are totally up to you.

If you keep the thought uppermost in your mind that work and personal life are totally separate, and how thick the line is between them is your business, and you are in control of this line, you'll be in good shape to become a winner at both.

Don't make things complicated, KISS = keep it simple stupid...JUST DO IT!

CHAPTER 29
SELF-MOTIVATION

Here is the section that is more like the "Pills in the bottle" that the doctor gives you to actually bring about a noticeable, outward behavior...CHANGE!

Remember the definition of learning? When information ACQUAIRED is APPLIED to the situation at hand to effect the desired change.

The following informational script contains the affirmations to actually bring about a major change in your belief system, and intern your outward behavior, which will of course make a major positive change in your relative income and earning potential.

That is IF, and only IF you listen to the recording you make of the script, on a daily basis for at least 10 to 15 days.

But...let's not get KARRRAAZZIE...try it for only 5 days consecutively, and see what happens. The subconscious mind is a very strange and also wonderful thing, but it IS just like a computer. Whatever you put into it, WILL come back to you much like a tape recorder, and very soon. So, be very careful of how you speak to yourself when you may do something that's not totally in your best interest.

You have two choices, one sounds like, "Your name....YOU IDIOT, HAVE YOU GOT A BRAIN IN YOUR HEAD AT ALL, OR YOU'RE JUST A RETARD, WHEN WILL YOU EVER LEARN THAT'S NOT THE WAY TO XXX"

Or in a much more positive vein,

"Your name...you could have done better this one time, and you get better all the time at making these types of decisions, you WILL do better next time, because you deserve the best life has to offer."

MAKING YOUR OWN MOTIVATIONAL REPROGRAMMING TAPE OR CD.

Everybody that offers a motivational course has got a motivational CD for you, which usually costs extra, but they tell you how beneficial it is to be able to "Take all the great info home with you."
So you buy it, and let sit in your "I'll get to this some day", file.

This is going to be a mental reprogramming recording CD, or cassette tape (yes some people still have cassettes). This means that it will effect a change in your belief system, which as you know if you've read the previous pages, is the seat of all your outward behavior. It is the reason you do the things you do, like the things you like, and attract the things that you now have; will have, and in general are the person you are when nobody's looking.

Your belief system is locked in your subconscious mind, the deeper part of you that has been discussed in earlier pages here, and once it has been programmed properly, it WILL give you the answers, and changes you are wanting in your outward and reactionary behavior. Reactionary behavior is defined as how you REact to unexpected situations and pressure. Is this behavior appropriate or are you thinking, "Why did I just do/say that"? Would like to have that moment to relive over again? We all have made those mistakes and wish we could have many moments to relive. This is about reducing those moments, eliminating many of those times when our mental computer was not only dysfunctional, but NON-functional, and giving us not only insufficient, but bad programming.

AXIOM OF CHANGE: Change the INSIDE first and the OUTSIDE will change automatically.

All you need is a recorder such as a small digital recorder, or even the audio recorder on your computer (you will need a sound card, and a microphone) some computers already have a built-in microphone. All is needed is something that will play back to you the sound you put into it.

Read the script just the way is written, and when doing the relaxation portion of the script, make adjustments to your voice in volume for example; when is says "As my voice gets softer, so do you go deeper and deeper into this drowsy state of

relaxation", let your voice volume drop with each word you speak.
LISTENING: Try to stay awake through the entire tape or cd, and make sure to do the visualizations that it tells you to imagine. When you fall asleep, the info still goes into your subconscious, but you don't get the benefit of the positive visualizations.

GENERAL INDUCTION SCRIPT TO BE READ INTO RECORDING DEVICE OR CD BURNER

NOTE: What you are creating here are commands for the subconscious mind to restructure your belief system. Therefore if you want to become relaxed use a "Relaxing" tone to your voice, draw out the word as in...
R E L A X...letting your voice drop and go softer at the end. Let your voice drop at the end of the sentence or word. The opposite is true, as in the awaking; put energy into your voice to instill energy in the listener (you) so you truly awaken with a new power and energy.

GENERAL INDUCTION SCRIPT

NOW I WANT YOU TO LAY BACK AND MAKE YOURSELF AS COMFORTABLE AS POSSIBLE, IN WHATEVER CHAIR, COUCH OR RECLINER YOU HAVE AVAILABLE. - I WANT YOU TO TAKE 3 DEEP BREATHS WITH ME AS I DO SO. NUMBER ONE (BREATHE IN SLOWLY...AND OUT SO THE RECORDER CAPTURES THE SOUND) NUMBER 2 (REPEAT) NUMBER 3 (REPEAT)
NOW YOU BEGIN TO FEEL A WONDERFUL NEW RELAXING POWER COMING OVER YOU STARTING A THE TOP OF YOUR HEAD, JUST DRAINING DOWN OVER YOUR FOREHEAD AS IT

GOES, JUST RELAXING YOUR FOREHEAD CAUSING YOU TO GO LOOSE...AND LIMP –
I AM GOING TO COUNT BACKWARD FROM 10 DOWN TO 1 AND WHEN I REACH 1 YOU'RE GOING TO BE IN A WONDERFUL NEW DEEP DEEP STATE OF AWARENESS TOTALLY RELAXED AND AT EASE.
NUMBER 10...YOUR FOREHEAD BECOMES LOOSE...AND LIMP...AND THE SKIN ON YOUR FORHEAD IS COMPLETELY SLACK AND LOOSE...AND LIMP. YOU KNOW IF YOUR FORHEAD IS RELAXED YOUR ENTIRE BODY IS RELAXED AND SO YOUR FORHEAD GOES LOOSE...AND LIMP...AND YOU ARE SO DROWSEY AND ARE BECOMING MORE RELAXED THE LONGER YOU LISTEN TO THE SOUND OF MY VOICE.

NUMBER 9 – THIS MAGICAL NEW RELAXING POWER IS NOW COMING OVER YOUR NECK A SHOULDER MUSCELS, JUST R-E-L-A-X-I-N-G YOUR NECK AND SHOULDER MUSCELS AS IT MOVES DOWN YOUR BODY
NUMBER 8 – THIS WONERFUL WARM BLANKET OF R-E-L-A-X-A-T-I-O-N (DRAW IT OUT) IS NOW MOVING INTO YOUR UPPER ARMS AND BICEPS BRINGING DEEP RELAXATION TO YOUR UPPER ARMS AND YOU GO DEEPER AND DEEPER INTO THIS WONDERFUL STATE OF DROWSEY R E L A X A T I O N
NUMBER 7 – NOW THIS POWERFUL WARM RELAXING POWER IS MOVING DOWN INTO YOUR LOWER ARMS AND YOUR FOREARMS BECOME SO LOOSE AND LIMP...AND YOU GO DEEPER DOWN INTO THIS WONDERFUL STATE OF DEEP...DEEP...R-E-L-A-X-A-T-I-O-N.
NUMBER 6 – THIS DEEP REALAXING POWER IS

NOW MOVING IN TO YOUR CHEST MUSCELS CAUSING YOU TO DRIFT DOWN DEEPER AND MORE RELAXED

NUMBER 5 – YOU FEEL THIS RELAXING POWER MOVING ACROSS THE BROAD MUSCELS OF YOUR BACK TAKING ALL THE TENSION AS IT GOES AND THESE MUSCELS GO LOOSE AND LIMP, YOU NOW FEEL SO AT EASE AND EVERY SOUND YOU HEAR MAKES YOU GO DEEPER AND DEEPER IN THE DROWSY STATE OF DEEP...DEEP

R-E-L-A-X-A-T-I-O-N

EACH AND EVERY TIME YOU LISTEN TO THESE WORDS YOU WILL GO DEEPER AND DEEPER, AND MORE RELAXED FASTER THAT THE TIME BEFORE.

NUMBER 4 – YOU FEEL THE RELAXING POWER NOW COMING IN YOUR STOMACH CAUSING YOU TO BECOME TOTALLY AT EASE MORE RELAXED THAN YOU'VE EVER BEEN...YOU GO DEEPER AND DEEPER

NUMBER 3 – THIS WARM BLANKET OF DEEP RELAXATION IS NOW MOVING INTO YOUR HANDS TOTALLY RELAXING YOUR HANDS AND ALL OF YOUR FINGERS

NUMBER 2 YOU FEEL THIS SAME WONDERFUL POWER MOVING DOWN IN TO YOUR LEGS, FIRST YOUR UPPER LEGS THEN YOUR LOWER LEGS AND CALVES TAKING ALL THE TENSION AS IT GOES, AND YOU GO DEEPER AND DEEPER IN DROWSY DEEP RELAXATION

ON THE NEXT COUNT YOU WILL BE THERE, IN THE DEEPEST STATE OF WONDERFUL RELAXATION YOU'VE EVER BEEN, TOTALLY AT PEACE, TOTALLY AT EASE AND YOU REALIZE YOU CAN COME OUT OF THIS WONDERFUL STATE OF DEEP RELAXATION ANY TIME YOU WISH FEELING REFRESHED AND ENERGIZED, BUT NOW YOU CHOOSE TO GO DEEPER AND MORE RELAXED THAT YOU'VE EVER

BEEN
EACH TIME I LISTEN TO THIS CD I GO FAR DEEPER MUCH FASTER AND I LOVE THIS FEELING OF DEEP RELAXATION, THIS IS MY REALITY.
NUMBER 1 – YOU'RE FINALLY THERE, TOTALLY RELAXED, TOTALLY AT EASE AND FEELING CENTERED AND CALM, NOW YOU WILL REMEMBER EVERY THING THAT HAS HAPPENED IN THIS SESSION AND ALLOW IT TO BE COMMITTED TO YOUR DEEPEST LEVEL OF BEING TO BE RELAYED TO ALL YOUR LEVELS OF AWARENESS.

Next is the reprogramming script that has the affirmations that will be implanted in the subconscious mind and begging to change the inward belief system that will ultimately change the outward behavior patterns.

NOW AS YOU GO DEEPER AND DEEPER INTO THIS DROWSEY STATE OF DEEP...DEEP...RELAXATION YOU ARE AWARE OF A NEW POWER AND STRENGTH COMING OVER YOU, IN THE AREA OF TALKING TO SALES CLIENTS AND NEW SALES PROSPECTS.

YOU ENJOY MAKING COLD CALLS AND GETTING THE OPPORTUNITY TO TALK AND RECEIVE DETAILED INFORMATION FROM YOUR PROSPECTIVE CUSTOMERS AND CLIENTS.

YOU ARE A MASTER AT LISTENING TO THEM AND RETAINING ALL THE INFORMATION THEY TELL YOU.

YOU ARE VERY ACCOMPLISHED AT REMEMBERING THEIR NAMES WHEN THEY TELL YOU THE FIRST

TIME. THIS IS YOUR NEW REALITY TO BE COMMUNICATED TO ALL YOUR LEVELS.

YOU ENJOY HELPING YOUR CUSTOMERS AND POTENTIAL CLIENTS TO GET EXACTLY WHAT THEY NEED AND THEY CAN SENSE YOUR HIGH LEVEL OF CONFIDENCE, AND YOU BOTH ENJOY A HIGH LEVEL OF RAPPORT WITH EACH OTHER.

YOU KNOW THAT THE UNIVERSE IS ABUNDANT AND SO YOU CLAIM YOUR FAIR SHARE OF THIS ABUNDANCE, AND ENJOY RETURNING SOME OF IT TO THE UNIVERSE TO BE USED AGAIN FOR PEOPLE WHO NEED HELP

I LOVE HELPING PEOPLE, AND THIS IS MY TRUE REALITY.

I LOVE HELPING PEOPLE AND THIS IS EASY TO SEE IN MY BEHAVIOR

ABUNDANCE IS MINE AND I ENJOY ABUNDANCE EACH AND EVERY DAY

I ENJOY ABUNDANCE EACH AND EVERY DAY
THIS IS MY REALITY COMMUNICATED TO ALL MY LEVELS AND TO MY DEEPEST LEVEL.

THE UNIVERSE IS ALWAYS ON MY SIDE, AND YOU FEEL SAFE AN STRONG. PEOPLE CAN SENSE THIS STRENGTH AND THEY LOOK TO ME FOR HELP AND GUIDANCE.

I AM A MONEY MAGNET ... I DRAW LARGER AND

LARGER SUMS OF MONEY AND OPPORTUNITY TO ME EACH DAY.

I GAIN MORE FINANCIAL KNOWLEDGE EACH DAY AND I ENJOY THIS KNOWLEDGE

I AM A MONEY MAGNET

NOW I AM GOING TO BEGIN TO SEE MYSELF IN A MENTAL MOVIE IN WHICH I CONTROL ALL THAT I SEE, HEAR AND FEEL. I AM GOING TO PICTURE MYSELF USING MY NEW FOUND POWERS TO DRAW NEW OPPORTUNITIES AND FINANCIAL SUCCESS TO ME LIKE A GIGANTIC MAGNET. I AM A MONEY MAGNET...I AM A MONEY MAGNET

I NOW AM GOING TO SEE MYSELF USING MY NEW POWERS TO DRAW THE WEALTH AND SECURITY TO ME VERY QUICKLY. I WILL SEE MYSLEF ENJOYING THE INTERACTION WITH MY CLIENTS AND CUSTOMERS, AND SEE MY SUCCESSFUL ACTIONS GAINING THEIR TRUST AND CONFIDENCE AND CLOSING MORE AND MORE BUSINESS.

I WILL DO THIS NOW IN THE NEXT FEW MINUTES OF SILENCE.

4 MINUTES OF DEAD SILENCE WITH THE TAPE OR RECORDER RUNNING

THERE, WHAT I HAVE JUST SEEN IS AN ACCURATE PROJECTION OF MY ABILITIES AS AN EXTREMELY EFFECTIVE SELLER OF MY PRODUCTS OR

SERVICES. THIS IS MY REALITY AND MY NEW FOUND POWER.

THIS IS COMMUNICATED TO ALL MY LEVELS AND MY DEEPEST LEVEL

STANDARD AWAKENING FOR ALL HYPNOSIS RECORDINGS
AWAKEING – THIS CAN – AND SHOULD - BE USED FOR ANY HYPNOSIS RECORDING

NOW IN A MIN. I AM GOING TO WAKE UP ..... I'M GOING TO COUNT FROM ONE TO FIVE AND WHEN I REACH 5 I AM GOING TO BE WIDE AWAKE SUPERCHARGED WITH A NEW POSITIVE ENERGY AND POWER TO TAKE ME THROUGH THE NEXT DAY OR EVENING.
NUMBER 1 ...YOU FEEL YOURSELF LETTING GO NOW, AND COMING BACK TO YOUR NORMAL STATE OF AWARENESS
NUMBER 2 ...YOU ARE BEGINNING TO FEEL LIKE YOUR BLOOD HAS BEEN DE-TOXIFIED, AND RE-ENERGIZED, FLOWING IN YOUR VEIGNS WITH A NEW POWER OF ENERGY, AND YOU LOVE THIS FEELING
NUMBER 3 ...YOU ARE RISING UP NOW LIKE A NUCLEIAR SUBMARINE BURSTING TO THE SURFACE OF THE WATER FROM DEEP BELOW THE OCEAN. REMEMBERING EVERYTHING THAT HAS TAKEN PLACE IN THIS SESSION.
NUMBER 4....ON THE NEXT COUNT YOU WILL BE WIDE AWAKE, SUPERCHARGED WITH A NEW

POSITIVE ENERGY AND AWARENESS, YOUR EYES FEEL LIKE THEY HAVE BEEN BATHED IN COOL SPRING WATER AND YOU FEEL WONDERFUL, READY TO BEGIN THE NEXT 12 HOURS

NUMBER 5...(CLAP YOUR HANDS LOUDLY)

YOU'RE WIDE AWAKE, ENERGIZED, AND FELLING WONDERFUL, READY TO REALIZE ALL THE BENEFITS YOU HAVE SEEN AND HEARD.

DISCLAIMER: Just for your info, don't record

ALWAYS ALLOW YOURSELF TO FULLY AWAKEN BEFORE ACCEPTING ANY RESPONSIBILITY, DRIVING, USING MACHINERY, CUTTING TOOLS, POWER TOOLS, OR ANYTHING WHERE A HIGHER LEVEL OF RESPONSIBILITY IS NECESSARY. YOUR SAFETY IS OF GREAT IMPORTANCE, LIFE IS NOT LIKE A VIDEO TAPE...THERE IS NO REWIND, NO REPLAY.

A Winners Way, Vector Studios accepts no responsibility for any negative occurrences associated with any of the mental reprogramming tape/CDs it produces, or instruction on how to produce mental reprogramming tapes/CDs.

SUBLIMINAL LEARNING

What is subliminal anyway? People have said many times, "I guess I just wanted it to happen subliminally, and that's why I screwed up"
Subliminal knowledge is like humility, if you know you have it...you don't' have it, and visa versa.

Subliminal means BELOW the level of conscious

awareness. Your conscious mind is not aware that you know the information, can repeat the information, and or relay that information outwardly.

It has been proven that people who have seen text upside down and backward still remember the message and can under hypnosis quote what their conscious mind could not remember.
Witnesses in criminal cases were hypnotized to remember a license number on a car as it sped away from the crime scene. The subconscious mind is a gigantic warehouse of information, feelings and belief system that we have little control over on a conscious level. That's why hypnosis is such a powerful tool in behavioral change and modification. So, if we could just keep the conscious mind from realizing what we are putting into our brains, it would go directly to the SUBconscious mind and eventually be filtered up to the conscious mind as a command that would change out outward behavior in that direction.

SLEEP LEARNING
While you are sleeping your conscious mind is at rest and you are open to suggestion and implantation of information to the subconscious. That's why sleep learning tapes were such a rage in the 70s, because physiologists discovered that people could retain vast amounts of information fed to them on a cassette tape played while in bed sleeping. That rage died out like a lot of other trendy stuff from the 60s/70s because people never continued to use it over and over again to allow it to work properly. It however, still works, it

is still the same phenomena, and can have the same effect on anyone that uses it. All you have to do is make sure that the affirmations and positive statements you are hearing are below the normal level of hearing for the environment you are in. On all the subliminal tapes that were created they put a "Mask" of sound over the actual wording. This would be soft music, the ocean, falling rain, anything to keep you from consciously hearing the words. You can do the same just by turning down the volume to keep you from fully understanding the wording all the time.

CREATING YOUR OWN SUBCONSCIOUS LEARNING CDs OR SUBLIMINAL TAPES

Keeping the idea in mind that all your deep inner mind (the subconscious) has to do, is receive the positive information over and over again to imprint it strongly, all you need to do is create this audio tape or CD and play it over and over again at a level just below the CONSCIOUS level of hearing.

An example would be having a CD or tape playing while driving down the road with the windows open, allowing the wind and highway noise to mask the UNDERSTANDABLE sound or words playing on that particular audio product. You regulate the volume of the audio to be just loud enough to hear the "Noise" but not consciously understand the words being said. So instead of actually HEARING, "Each day when I get up I feel

a great level of strength and happiness all around me", you hear..."Eah dzz whkj lkjsdf afjlksajfee serentjlkj j happnljlkjlkj blachl, lkj"
Because you did not CONSCIOUSLLY UNDERSTAND the words, the message was absorbed by your subconscious mind and still remains there forever. The more you "Listen" to the CD the stronger the reprogramming becomes, and finally you begin to notice how you feel about this aspect of yourself that you want to change. You can play it while doing any task where you need to consciously THINK and to focus intently on one thing, in order to accomplish it without a mistake. All you have to do is OCCUPY your conscious mind totally and anything heard, seen or felt goes directly to the SUBconscious mind.

As it has been stated before the subconscious is the seat of all your outward behavior, and as you well know sometimes you do things that are not in your best interests, and you keep banging your head against the wall trying to understand why.
All you need to do REPROGRAM this guidance system and then just relax and let your amazing computer do the work. What we are talking about here is how to make a tool to reprogram this computer.
Just imagine, if you were to hear the words, "I enjoy cold calling because it gives me a chance to meet new clients that will turn in to sales", 25 times in 15 minutes, but in the background, and

have it go into your mental computer.

Because your mind (according to Russian research) is capable of thinking or assimilating data 5 times faster than you can talk, you brain can absorb this info with ease.

So, now your only challenge is to write a script that you can read into a recording device that will play back to you that info repeatedly. It doesn't need to be a long drawn out or involved speech, just simple commands that will go into your mental computer, and WILL change your behavior to be the "NEW" PERSON you want to be.

So, here is a good script to start with:

I ENJOY TALKING TO PEOPLE

COLD CALLING IS FUN

EACH DAY I GET BETTER AT LISTENING

I ENJOY LEARNING ABOUT PEOPLE

I DESERVE THE BEST LIFE HAS TO OFFER

THIS IS MY REALITY

I ENJOY HELP MY CLIENTS

EACH DAY I BECOME BETTER AT WHAT I DO

I DESERVE WEALTH AND PROPERITY

I DRAW MONEY TO ME LIKE A MAGNET I AM A MONEY MAGNET

PEOPLE ENJOY BEING WITH ME

I AM A GOOD PERSON

THIS IS MY REALITY

I LOVE LIFE AND DESERVE THE BEST

THE UNIVERSE IS ABUNDANT FOR ALL

I ENJOY LIFE AND MAKING MONEY

Read this into a recorder about 5 times so that it

repeats over and over again for the entire cd. If you use a cd it will automatically repeat without having to create a lot of tracks, actually repeating each one over and over again.

SUGGESTED PLAYBACK

Since the act of reprogramming the subconscious is REPETITION, put this cd into your automobile cd player and keep it on so that when you start the engine it begins to play immediately. Pretty soon it will be playing all the time in the background; you won't even notice it, which is the way it should be. The programming should always be present for about two weeks. Even after a week you will begin to notice the difference in your behavior, and your results in your behavioral change.

Remember this is taking place without any actual work on your part; this is what they call "Passive" behavioral change, and passive learning.

All you have got to do is LISTEN, or actually push a button to activate the cd and have it going in the background.

REMEMBER, *there is no motivational CD to MAKE you play the motivational CD!*

At some point you have to put it in the player, hit play and adjust the volume so you can "Almost" understand the words, and remain in the general vicinity.

CHAPTER 30
WHAT DOES IT ALL MEAN?

A good friend of mine and I would have lengthy conversations of why there was a Universe, how God figured into "Things", why there was gravity, how they figured out the "Quantum theory", how we could figure the patterns of winning the lotto, and why the other salespeople we knew kept "Shooting themselves in the foot".

Somewhere along the line of exhaustive babbling and theorizing he would always come up with the phrase, "Well, what does it all mean?"

So that is the question you have to ask yourself, "What does it all mean?" What is the "IT" to you? Is it to make a ton of money, and if that's your focus, ask why DO you need a *ton* of money?

Someone said "What's the point of making a ton of money, so you can work harder than you ever have in your life to keep the Government and other people from taking it."

Now you have to pay an accountant a considerable portion of that ton of money, to keep you from paying more taxes, because you made more money than you really needed, to buy things you didn't really want, to impress people you didn't really like!

So, what DOES it all mean? Everyone needs to from time to time step back, and take a good

"Evaluation look" at themselves, their life, their family's life, who their friends are and how they relate to the world and what's happening around them.

Also how much they are contributing to our society as a whole, and how much good this money (that they're working so hard to earn) is doing for them and the ones around them.

HAPPINESS VARIABLE

So ask yourself the big question, "How happy am I?" Do you spend more time worrying about "New Stuff", rather than enjoying the old stuff (that used to be new stuff) you already have?

How important is that stuff, and how much of it could you just let go of if you wanted to be really free. Does it really matter if you have a new or "NewER" car, boat, plane, or whatever makes you temporarily "Happy"? Are "Things" more important to you that relationships, friends, and health?

Are you in the kind of sales that actually helps people do a better job of whatever they do, or makes their life better, easier, or more fulfilled?

There is no greater feeling that to have a satisfied customer/client walk out the door or get off the phone, and know that you've made their life a little bit better, improved their quality of life, and brought a little ray of sunshine their way, by your efforts.

Sales is a very rewarding profession, and it gives you a chance to change someone's life by leading them in the right direction, toward something that they need or thought they needed, and this should make you, or anyone else for that matter feel like they've done something worthwhile.

Finally it comes down to much more than just how much money you make, what kind of car you drive or how many vacations a year you take. It's what have you done with your time on the Earth, how well have you used this precious commodity we call time.

Has it been all about us, and making OUR life better, more luxurious, more fun, more recreational, or have we spent some of this time to help someone, or improve things on our planet.

You'd be surprised how much force and power you have when your reasoning for making extra money is backed by needing it to help someone else.

In quoting from the book by Michael Phillips author of "The Seven Laws of Money", he says, "You can never give money away". He goes on to say that money is part of a two way flow, and basically you push (or give to someone else) money into the Universe, and that push you just enacted, causes the flow to direct BACK to you even more money than you gave.

I can tell you this is a very powerful and TRUE statement. Every time I've given money to a homeless person on the street corner, or put it in the collection plate at church, it has come back to ME many times over.

So in the spirit of "What does it all mean", think of what you can do with some of this extra cash you'll be getting by using the concepts in this book. Think of the positive results it will bring about when you put it to good use to help someone else less fortunate that yourself.

It is said that we were put here on this earth to seek JOY, but you can't GET joy unless you give it to begin with. How do you give it? Help someone in some way when you know you will not be paid in dollars and cents.

Sometimes it's more than just forking over a few bucks to a needy cause, or loaning a friend some money, but actually putting out some energy in a positive direction, like volunteering for a Habitat project, or agreeing to pick up some groceries for a bed ridden person in a home.

Or just doing something good for someone that you know needs help, with absolutely no expectation of anything in return.

You decide how you would like to "Give back" and then JUST DO IT. Suddenly your sales will go through the roof, it will seem like you're getting all the lay downs, and you WILL get this great feeling of "I am contributing to the Universe of help". You can't buy JOY like that, you can't manufacture the feeling you get from helping someone become better than they are, and you ALWAYS will be rewarded for your efforts in teaching someone a way to achieve more money, a better job, and eventually a better life.

HELP AXIOM: *Every time you help someone you help yourself, and every time you hurt someone you hurt yourself.*
If in every sale you make, you feel you've done the best you can at getting the customer/client what they needed for the price that was fair and justified, you are putting a shot of positive energy into the Universe, and IT WILL COME BACK TO YOU!

Never forget the OPPOSITE is also true. If you cheat someone, sell them something you know is faulty, for a price that is inflated, and take advantage of their lack of knowledge or experience, you will be repaid in like kind.

AND, I wouldn't want to be you when the Universe "Comes knock'in" to extract payment, and it *WILL* come. The trouble is, sometimes it's very poor at extracting from you the correct amount in relationship to that last deal you pulled on someone, so it just may take 10 times what you actually "Owe" in money you made. By the same token it may GIVE you 10 times what you deserve when you've helped someone, taught them a skill or some way to make their life better.

The Universe is self-leveling, self-maintaining, and sometimes not fair, but ALWAYS GIVES back to you, or gets BACK AT YOU, for what you put in.

My last words in advice to you are:

BE CAREFUL!

Don't ask why...

JUST DO IT!

About the Author

Roger W. Breternitz – CCht.
Salesman, Author, Lecturer, Trainer

A graduate of Illinois State University with a degree in Education and Southern Illinois University in design and graphics, he makes his home in Laguna Niguel, California. With certifications in clinical hypnotherapy and Neuro Linguistic Programming he is currently presenting lectures and seminars on the art of sales and quality communication for corporations and sales organizations wanting to improve their profit margin and inter-office harmony.

His sales career spans 36 years in many different venues dealing with a multitude of products and services along with benefiting from the sales training of many of these organizations, and a variety of gurus and trainers. It is from this experience, training and educational courses that he derives his expertise, and insight to produce the book, "Winning at Sales". He hopes it will shorten your learning curve in the use of new and more effective presentation and closing techniques, along with giving you the tools necessary to quickly become the top salesperson in your chosen field.

The best of luck in your quest to reach the top, and never forget the winner's creed, "JUST DO IT!"

Thanks for your interest,

Roger W. Breternitz CCht.

Web site:http://www.awinnersway.com

Other publications: Winning, It's a Lot More Fun! By Roger W. Breterntiz CCht. Copyright 2012 – Vector Studios

www.ingramcontent.com/pod-product-compliance
Lightning Source LLC
Chambersburg PA
CBHW060146200526
45165CB00023B/105
* 9 7 8 1 4 8 2 3 3 7 6 6 2 *